The Agony of the Kemalist Republic and the Rise of a Fascist Brotherhood of the Corrupt, by the Corrupt, for the Corrupt

The Agony of the Kemalist Republic and the Rise of a Fascist Brotherhood of the Corrupt, by the Corrupt, for the Corrupt

Sedat Sami

To order additional copies of this book, contact:
Xlibris Corporation
1-888-795-4274
www.Xlibris.com
Orders@Xlibris.com

75403

CONTENTS

To Mehmetçik

PREFACE

If a nation expects to be ignorant and free, it expects what never was and never will be.

—*Thomas Jefferson*

Corrupt and bankrupt regimes of today evoke in most Turks the corrupt sultans of yesteryears. Indeed, theirs ought to serve us as a reminder of the dreadful consequences of corruption in high places. For the present leaders of Turkey, the path that lead the mighty Ottoman Empire from greatness to the dustbin of history is a good place to look for the early signs of decadence and eventual perdition. Historian H. C. Armstrong[1] gave us a sobering picture of a nation ending bankrupt, decrepit, and rotting:

> Sultan Sulyman the Magnificent, the Law-Giver, ruled with justice and strength an immense empire which stretched from Albania on the Adriatic coast to the Persian frontier, from Egypt to the Caucasus . . . In 1580 he hammered on the gates of Vienna and seized Christendom by the throat.

He failed, and after him came corruption.

> . . . After him, with one exception, came twenty-seven sultans each more degenerate than the last.

> . . . Without leaders the Turks went the way of all flesh. The steel fibre went out of them. Their energy, hardiness and vitality disappeared. They became corrupt in blood and morals.

> . . . Within three hundred years of the greatness of Sulyman the Magnificent, the Ottoman Empire lay bankrupt, decrepit and rotting.

Atatürk derided the decadent, corrupt state of the old regime and appealed to the honor and destiny of the Turkish people. Together they forged a powerful union and built a republic on the ashes of the empire. That was the genesis of the Kemalist revolution. And yet today we are witnessing a creeping Islamist countermovement slowly eroding the gains of that era. From all corners of the political arena, reactionary forces are attempting to sap the foundations of the secular republic. Kemalism—this poorly understood and just as poorly appreciated movement that pulled the Turkish nation from ending bankrupt, decrepit, and rotting again—has become a practice target for modern-day Islamists; reactionary leftists; politically correct Western media who never miss a chance to criticize Atatürk, the soldier, national hero, and statesman; and the Turkish Armed Forces who stood guard in defense of the Kemalist reforms. Fortunately, many came to regret their early opposition and said so openly. "I feel ashamed to have criticized Atatürk in my youth!" confessed Aziz Nesin, writer and humorist.

This book aims, first, to reach to the American public at large and explain in great detail the merits of a series of reforms that saved the nation from national humiliation. It also aims at educating adequately and informing accurately the international public about the seriousness of Turkey's slide into the abyss.

Four years ago, I wrote that "[w]hen corruption has metastasized within the body politics, social justice rings hollow, corporations are controlled by a web of vested interests, and people with neither shame nor conscience rob the nation's patrimony and destroy its social and economic fabric, it is fair to say that the future of the nation is cloudy."[2] In a broader sense, this book represents a sequel to the previous one. It documents the corrosive influence of the international finance when it links up with local oligarchs and feudal lords to gain control of the country's major industries and infrastructures.

While researching for the various fields in which Turkey has stagnated or even regressed, I was saddened to note the severity of the degradation of the Turkish public education system. It has been and continues to be one area where Turkey's future hangs in the balance. I am reminded of what Thomas Jefferson once said,[3]

> Enlighten the people and tyranny and oppression of body and
> mind will vanish like spirits at the dawn of day.

The present Islamist regime is hell-bent on desecularizing the state public education system and streamlining it with religious education disguised under the general curriculum of ethics. Disregarding all the various branches of Islam, this regime, true to its Naqshibendi brotherhood tilt, has fashioned the religious curriculum to fit its Sunni-Wahhabi-Naqshibendi teaching, thus leaving no choice to the Shiites, the Alawites, and all other subdenominations of Islam.

The Islamist imprint on theTurkish national public education has had another very nefarious result. The education of girls, particularly in the eastern part of the country where poverty is endemic, received lip sevice, leaving them mostly at home, thus depriving them from advancing through high schools and universities. Women empowerment in Turkey is an area that has become symptomatic of the true nature of the social depravation caused by this regime.

Despite having the 17th largest economy in the world, Turkey remains low on development indices due to the condition of women in the country. Turkey ranks 129th out of 134 countries in terms of women's economic and social conditions. It is 79th on the development index. These are numbers that should put to shame any political leadership. For the Islamists, the place of the woman being at home, these numbers do not cause even a ripple. With the prime minister calling women every day to reproduce—"at least three children!"—it is hard for the country to enter the twenty-first century with an educated and well-trained workforce.

The gathering of evidence and the collection of data necessarily relies on both personal observations as well as published documents and articles. The Turkish media has lately become rather tame and timid, having lost some of its most courageous voices to the blatant intimidation of the regime, which has become very efficient in using both carrot and stick. The powerful religious holdings, underwriting the publications that are nothing more than their masters' voices, have grabbed almost two-thirds of all media outlets, thus silencing independent reporting and analysis. Reliance on the reporting and analysis of the international media has always been risky. Many bring their own baggages with, and for an untrained reader seeking unvarnished and fair reporting, the challenge is great. Nevertheless, I am grateful to all those who joined me in preparing this manuscript, including the men and women of the media and my friends and colleagues all across Turkey and the United States. They all gave me their best advice.

I have particularly enjoyed the collaboration and selfless help of the people at Xlibris. It is a pleasure to thank K.E. Reroma, M.J. Pino, S. Daniels, CB Coleman and Jeremy Baring for their valuable guidance and generous support.

Turks are brave and generous people. But unfortunately, for many years, they have proven to be most inept at choosing their leaders. Now it is proving to be a rather costly shortcoming. I am confident that eventually common sense will prevail; and Turks, young and old, will rise up and defend what was, and still is, their most valuable asset: their independent and secular Kemalist republic.

PROLOGUE

*The tree of liberty must be refreshed from time to time with the
blood of patriots and tyrants.*
—*Thomas Jefferson*

About three years ago, the use and abuse of Islam in Turkish politics
and the threat Islamists posed the future of the Kemalist republic was dealt
with in a book detailing the fundamentalist Islam's inroads into the secular
foundations of the regime.[4] Since then, the nation has voted and, on July 22,
2007, renewed, overwhelmingly, the mandate of the governing party. The
results surprised many, but not everybody. Indeed, the government's claim
of an economic miracle was accepted at face value. The international media,
enamored with the free market economy of the Islamist regime, had even
coined the term Anatolian Tigers to describe the Islamic businesses sprouting
all over the heartland of conservative Anatolia. And yet, in the words of a
foreign observer, the governing party was engaged in an "economic Potemkin
village charade." Now, eight years later, we have the very words of the
proud owner of one of these "tigers": "We were Anatolian Tigers, we have
become Anatolian Donkeys!" What's more, an endemic political corruption
is threatening the economy as well as the social fabric of the nation. Rampant
cases of kickback, bribery, theft and fraud by government and party officials
are routinely reported, though they are ignored regularly.

The same can be said of another myth frequently offered by the Islamist
regime: that Turkey is a fully functioning democracy. The fundamentalist wing of
the party, in alliance with a greed-driven business oligarchy and a male-dominant
feudal culture, deprives the public of an enlightened understanding of what a
democracy is. All relevant policies and their likely consequences are hidden
from the public, and instead, a virtual world of make-believe democracy is
played before the eyes of an ill-informed citizenry. In such a "democracy,"
the governing party will deliver, just before national elections, tons of coal to
households—even when it is the middle of the summer and even if some are
using natural gas for heating. In such a "democracy," the governing party will
issue, just prior to national elections, national health insurance cards to millions
of its citizens. In such a "democracy," the governing party will promise, just

before national elections, the ultimate clincher: to revise the constitution and allow the wearing of the headscarf in state universities.

That Turkey is an underdeveloped democracy must be the first issue in need of clarification. Too much has been said about the U.S. policy in the Middle East and the role the U.S. neocons had assigned to the "moderate Islamic republic" of Turkey. Turkey was supposed to be the ideal role model for all the Arab theocracies and autocracies. The Turkish regime's willingness to play the part was predicated upon her hope of securing protection against any future Kemalist and/or military intervention and an understanding view, by the United States, of the Islamist regime's slow but steady move toward an Islamic society and away from the republic's secular roots.

The Kemalist institutions established by the republic, including and especially the Turkish Armed Forces, have never been the favorites of the Islamists—the Naqshibendis, the Fethullah Gülen brotherhood, the promoters of the so-called Second Republic, and the old leftists who are the neoliberals of George Soros. Recently, Nobel laureate Orhan Pamuk—who, ever since he established residence in New York City and began lecturing at Columbia University, has become a regular of the *Charlie Rose Show*—has added his pedigree to the above list of the enemies of the secular Republicans. They will all tell you that the secular forces are not true democrats, and that they "do not respect human rights!"

First and foremost, let's set the record straight: All Turkish institutions are institutions of the republic. Even those sold and privatized for a fraction of their true values and grabbed by friendly oligarchs of the regime are products of the Kemalist revolution.

Surely, Kemalism has been the founding ideology of the republic. However, Kemalism did not follow the footsteps of a public declaration of principles and intention, a manifesto. Kemalism was and still is a user's guide to enable the republic in its march forward. Such a user's guide is not and cannot be a collection of reactionary principles. On the contrary, it represents a revolutionary program. It consists of eight fundamental laws, which laid the foundations of the Kemalist republic and are the main targets of those who make a sport out of attacking, insulting, disparaging the guardians of those so-called laws of the revolution.

So it is appropriate at this time to ask them to clarify a few points:

- The law establishing a unitary educational system. Would you be in favor of dual-track schooling? Would you like to see some youngsters attending Shariah schools (madrassa) while others attend regular state-run secular schools?

- The law abolishing the wearing of certain headgears. Would you favor a return to the days when the fez was the main headgear for men?
- The law abolishing all religious orders, fraternities, brotherhoods (*tariqat, tekke*). Would you like to see them operate even "more openly" than they do at the present with a total disregard for the law?
- The law abolishing the practice of the Shariah as the law of the land. Banning polygamy and requiring the officiating of marriage to be carried out by an officer of the law. How would you like to live under the Shariah?
- The law adopting the Western numerals, which are a modified form of the Arabic numerals.
- The law adopting a modified version of the Latin alphabet, although many Islamists would like to read and write in the alphabet of the Qur'an.

The law abolishing certain honorary titles such as effendi, bey, pasha. Some, nevertheless, are still in daily use although they are not honorific.

- The law prohibiting the wearing of certain clothing such as the burka, the veil. Would you be interested in wearing them? Although many pious women are today freely parading around with the full complement of black robe and veil and in total contravention of the law?

So what is the fuss about the Kemalist revolution, unless it is a subtle attempt to scuttle the whole idea of a secular way of life?

Another important issue has been with the republic ever since the regime moved to a multiparty system and, almost immediately, surrendered to the pressures of international finance organizations—World Bank (WB) and International Monetary Fund (IMF)—and accepted to live (and die) by the rules of a savage capitalism disguised as "free market economy" and regulated by the high priests of globalization, liberalization, privatization. That is when the selling of Turkey began in earnest and, apparently, will continue until there is nothing left to sell.

Nevertheless, neither of these two issues could have gained traction if not for the betrayal of Atatürk's legacy by men and women collaborationists lured by the money and power of both internal as well as external institutions serving the interests of their respective masters. The end result of such a Faustian bargain was to legitimize, in the eyes of an ill-informed public, the policies of a regime fundamentally corrupt and inept.

Eventually, the coup de grâce to the legacy of the Kemalist republic was administered when a toxic brew began to dominate the national landscape: a corrupt political elite, an equally corrupt business oligarchy, dominant religious orders and brotherhoods, and tribal chiefs of an entrenched feudal society still ruling in the southeast, all jockeying for power and anxious for a piece of the action. They are the poison of any free and democratic society, the rot that would eventually bring down the house of any nation.

However, the threat to the Turkish Republic has another dimension. The house that Kemal Atatürk founded rests on a foundation called a nation-state. Atatürk was fully aware of the multiethnic character of the nation. His efforts to nationalize such a diverse multiethnic society by successfully integrating the various component groups of the Ottoman Empire into a common Turkish identity has been one of his crowning achievements. Now we are witnessing internal and external challenges not only to the notion of Kemalism as a reformist movement but also to the very essence of the republic as a nation-state. The Kurdistan Workers' Party (PKK) has, for over thirty years, waged a savage war of terrorism against the civilian population in order to gain autonomy for the Kurdish region of Turkey. As for the external challenges faced by the republic, the most insidious has been, for the last decade, the demands of the European Union aimed at removing the Turkish Armed Forces from its position of guardianship of the Kemalist reforms and, in particular, of the secular nature of the Turkish Republic.

In what follows, the ills sapping the social fabric and the economic and political strength of the republic are discussed. Successive generations of political leaders have failed the nation. The demagogues and the false prophets of Turkish politics and the modern-day robber barons of business, in cahoots with the commissars of the European Union, have never been more threatening. A deeply ingrained habit of "pay for play," a pervasive gender inequality and a lack of serious commitment to education are undermining the resolve of the Republic to fight back. The hope is, as always, the nation's resilience and its capacity to fight fiercely when faced with lethal danger. Turkey has been served notice: the enemies are closing in. A day of reckoning is upon us.

1

Existential Crisis

Debt and Death

> *There are two ways to conquer and enslave a nation. One is by sword, the other is by debt.*
>
> —*John Adams*

History never lies. That is why successful leaders will always consider the lessons of history before embarking upon any major course of action that might risk to be injurious to the safety and security of their nation. But in order to learn from a historical event, we need to pay attention to the underlying causes precipitating it and identify similarities and parallels between the past and the present. Turkey's present-day predicament offers a striking similarity to that of its predecessor, the Ottoman Empire. The decline of the empire can be quite accurately traced to a fifty-year period beginning with the 1830 commerce and navigation treaty signed with the United States and followed by the infamous Treaty of Balta Liman signed in 1838 with Britain on the grand vezir's private residence located along the Bosporus.

Article 1 of the commerce and navigation treaty accorded the United States the "most favored nation" status whereas Article 4 recognized for U.S. citizens the same rights and privileges accorded by the Ottoman Empire to all other European nationals. Such rights and privileges eventually became the albatross around the neck of the Ottoman State and were referred to as the Capitulations.

The 1838 treaty signed with Britain may be called a watershed accord. The events leading to the treaty are illustrative of how the Ottoman Empire's inability to suppress a rebellion—in Egypt—led to the capitulation of the sultan to the demands of Britain. In fact, following the treaty, Britain had gained free access to Turkish internal commerce. Moreover, the treaty accorded British citizens tax advantages not available to local citizenry. Of course, such lucrative trade advantages could not have been limited to British merchants for too long: similar treaties followed with France, Spain, Holland, and a few others. The nightmare called the Capitulations would not be abolished before the last nail was placed on the coffin of the Ottoman Empire.

Let us fast-forward to December 1995 when then prime minister Tansu Çiller was proudly affixing her signature to a treaty signed between Turkey and the European Union (EU) and referred to as the Customs Union. It removed all custom restrictions to the movement of goods between the parties. But there was a catch: it did not cover essential economic areas, such as agriculture and services. Stripped from its veneer, the Customs Union wide-opened the Turkish market to European industrial goods but restricted the free shipment of Turkish agricultural produces into the European Union. Even on items where Turkey had a strong position in world markets, such as textiles, import quotas were enforced. Today, almost fifteen years after the Customs Union came into effect, the picture, as far as Turkey is concerned, is as bleak as can be. Indeed, in a report prepared by the Turkish Civil Service Union's Research and Development Center, it was noted that the average annual trade deficit, which was $7.6 billion between the years 1987 and 1995, has ballooned to an average of $19.7 billion for the period 1996-2004. The obvious consequence of the Custom Union has been to make Turkey a big and lucrative market for the goods of EU member states while depriving Turkish farmers from competing on an equal footing with the goods produced within the EU or imported from the former colonies of some EU member states.

The consequences of Turkey's total capitulation to the diktat of international capital has been slow to emerge. Yes, unemployment was inching up; yes, nation's fiscal health appeared to get worse by the month, but nevertheless, the public passively watched. A certain moral, social, and economic disintegration slowly was gaining strength, further aggravated by any absence of moral outrage on the part of a public that appeared to have been sedated by the national and international media. Especially nefarious was the role played by the international media in the propping up a particularly corrupt and incompetent regime. Partly due to their ignorance of the historical background surrounding current events they were reporting about and partly due to their own bias, the international media seemed to have adopted this regime. In their eyes, the litmus test for the success of a regime had always been its ability to serve its wealthy supporters in showcase shopping malls where the reporters would discover, to their delight, a Dolce&Gabbana, a Starbucks, or some other upscale symbol of Western consumerism. For these reporters, a "laissez-faire, laissez-passer" economy in its most obscene form would not be cause for the slightest ripple of criticism.

A reader would have to look elsewhere to learn about a country where 41 percent of women have no primary education diploma, where only a third of young people attend high school, where youth unemployment is above 30 percent, where two-thirds of those participating in university entrance exams fail admission, and over one million street children are in need of attention.

Ever since the 1980s' so-called reforms initiated by the late president Turgut Özal, Turkey has been the victim of a "trust-cartel" economy that created a handful of mega billionaires and millionaires and, in return, saddled the nation's future generations with an unbearable debt burden. The interest Turkish treasury paid (1980-2007) on that debt is a staggering $450 billion. During the same period, the total amount invested was less than $100 billion. Worse yet, during the multiparty period (1960-1980) preceding the Özal era of privatization, the Turkish currency had depreciated about fivefold or 500 percent. Whereas during the next twenty years (1980-2000), Özal era economic policies reduced the value of the currency by a whopping eight-thousandfold or 800,000 percent. During the past five years, the interest paid on the debt, at times, reached the incredible sum of a billion dollars per week! Finally, it is necessary to remind international observers that when the interest rate was hovering around 18-20 percent, Turkey was the darling of hot-money investors worldwide until the recent international financial crisis.

The present Islamist regime's answer to the nation's enormous debt problem was to borrow a page from the Ottoman Sultan's solution to his 1870s debacle. Recep Tayyip Erdoğan (RTE) government balanced the budget by borrowing abroad and accumulating huge domestic and foreign debts. It then tried to cope with this massive external debt crisis by selling off revenue streams to foreign investors. The outward appearance of an affluent society, particularly in large urban centers, was maintained by opening up all gates to multinational corporations and flooding the market with import goods. In fact, the importation of luxury goods had been the most lucrative form of business, and for a businessman, the easy way to enrich oneself was to sell his/her business to multinational corporations. The above situation is further exacerbated by the fact that individuals, companies, and institutions routinely ignore the common good. Worse yet, for intellectuals, writers, and artists, the most direct route to international acclaim was through insulting and tearing down the nation's historical heritage and praising the multinationals' inroads into the national economy. In the words of a political commentator, "Turkish ruling classes reminds one of the ship captain busily tearing down and burning the cabin walls in order to keep the warmth going."

Illiberal Democracy

Religion as an instrument of foreign policy, whether it serves the purpose of fighting communism in Afghanistan against the Soviet Union or as a Trojan horse—in the case of Turkey—to achieve democratic reforms in the

Arab Middle East, has always been viewed by the foreign media through pink lenses.

So, here too, in order to predict the future trend, it is highly useful to observe and compare historic trends in nations with similar afflictions. Pakistan, a state that some are tempted to qualify as being on the verge of failing, is a case in point. Radical Islam never blossoms overnight. Rather, it germinates in an ideological landscape fertilized by the actions of populist politicians playing the Islamic card. Indeed, both Pakistani and Turkish politicians, in need of recharging their failing legitimacy, have unhesitatingly and shamelessly resorted to make Islam their reference point.

Such progression takes place on a slippery slope. There is seldom an opportunity to stop at midcourse. The path taken by past leaders of Pakistan is quite revealing: The founding father's secular leaning notwithstanding, those who followed Ali Jinnah were in need of Islam in order to solidify their grip to power. In later years—'70s—another leader, Zulfikar Ali Bhutto, and his Pakistan Peoples Party (PPP) proved to be better in adopting populist policies regardless of their consequences as long as they help them win votes. Bhutto, among other things, embarked in the formation of the Organisation of the Islamic Conference(OIC) and, in a desperate appeal to the Islamic roots of the nation, attacked the Ahmadi sect by accusing them of apostacy. Finally, by rigging the national elections, he precipitated his own downfall.

He was followed in this race by Zia-ul-Haq, a military coup leader who made the Islamic alms (*zekat*) compulsory and augmented tenfold the number of madrassas, where future generations of radical Islamists got their first taste of Islamic jihadism. It was claimed, of course, that such measures have always been advocated and adopted for the purpose of neutralizing the role of religious parties in the political life of the nation. But the fact of the matter is that they, on the contrary, helped the Islamization of the society to a degree unknown before. Most institutions and even the army succumbed to this reactionary evolution of the society. According to Ahmed Rashid, many of Pakistan's current "problems—the militancy of religious parties, the mushrooming of madrassas and extremist groups, the spread of drug and Kalashnikov culture, and the increase in secterian violence—took place during the Zia era."[5]

Revisionist historians would like us to believe that the Talibanization of Afghanistan was in response to the Soviet occupation and was helped by the CIA when, in reality, the Taliban was nothing more than a creature of the Pakistan Secret Services desirous of maintaining in the neighboring regions of Afghanistan a Pashtun-dominated regime pliant and friendly to Pakistan.

The Islamization of the Kemalist republic, sadly, had followed a similar path during its journey into the darkness:

> the death of Kemal Atatürk and the end of World War II, the trend to reverse the earlier achievements of the revolution began in earnest. The footsteps of the counter-revolution could be heard clearly following the general elections of 1946, during which the opposition "Demokrat" Party exploited the religious sensitivities of the public, and especially of the rural population. Gripped with a sense of panic, the party that always laid claim to the mantle of Atatürk began to dismantle, in quick succession, the various segments of the edifice that he had painstakingly built.

> It began in the area of education, with the introduction of religious courses, the reopening of the imam-hatip schools, and the inauguration of faculties of theology in the universities . . .

> The multi-party system became a race to the bottom, and parties competed to prove that they could deliver the most religious programs to the voters.[6]

Thus, the Turkish political establishment was surrendering not only to the lords of Western capitalism through the rules imposed upon by the IMF and WB, but it was also surrendering—in the true meaning of the word "Islam"—to a political ideology bent on destroying the secular republic. In the case of Turkey, the only remaining question is whether or not the Turkish Islamist regime too has crossed its point of no return.

Political Islam is a reactionary-fundamentalist movement that has nothing to do with a religious belief. It is essentially a political ideology without an economic model of its own. Throughout the Middle East and Southeast Asia, such a model always relies on a market economy that is not always free but is always mounted on an autocratic and/or theocratic regime.

In a nutshell, the two-headed monster described above illustrates the nature of the existential crisis facing Turkey today. Fareed Zakaria, observing the fact that not all elections point to a free and democratic society, has called the outcome "illiberal democracy."[7] Quoting the American diplomat Richard Holbrooke, who, on the eve of the 1996 Bosnian elections, was describing his nightmare scenario as one where "the election was declared free and fair but the winners were racists, fascists, separatists." Fareed Zakaria concludes that "from Peru to the Palestinian Authority, from Sierra Leone to Slovakia, from

Pakistan to the Philippines, we see the rise of a disturbing phenomenon in international life—illiberal democracy."

The classical definition of "democracy" calls for a system of constitutional and representative government in which those who would wield power can be dismissed and replaced without violence and by known rules and procedures universally understood and accepted. According to Samuel Huntington, this must happen at least twice before democracy can be regarded as consolidated.[8] Which is a rather dubious criteria, given the fact that the late Turkish prime minister Adnan Menderes was reelected in 1954 by a landslide and again in 1957 in a rather questionable fashion before ruining the economy and becoming, by 1961, an absolute autocrat who was brought down by a military coup.

The above definition is further qualified by Bernard Lewis, who would require the presence of a "civil society" for the proper functioning of a representative democracy.[9] Obviously, Bernard Lewis could not have imagined the *alla turca* version of his "civil society," which, in Turkey, includes all religious orders, brotherhoods, and the like. All indeed ready and willing to corrupt the established secular structure of the state for the benefit of a political ideology, i.e., political Islam.

The question remains, Is it possible to create democracy and tolerate political Islam, which rejects the notion of the sovereignty of the people and thus represents the complete antithesis of the secular Western democracy?

Indeed, the present Turkish prime minister Recep Tayyip Erdoğan, during his early years as mayor of Istanbul, challenged the right of the modern Turkish nation-state to its citizens' absolute loyalty. He liked to remind his audiences that it is the omnipotent deity, Allah, who is entitled to his final loyalty. "Sovereignty belongs to Allah!" he used to declare, contrasting it with what is written on the parliament's mural: "Sovereignty belongs unconditionally to the nation."

The U.S. Supreme Court seems to have offered the most succinct answer to the above question in a ruling related to the practice of polygamy. It stated that to permit a person to practice his/her religious duty in the presence of a strict prohibition "would be equivalent to make the professed doctrines of religious belief superior to the laws of the land, and in effect to permit every citizen to become a law unto himself." In such a circumstance, the court concluded, "The government could exist only in name."[10] It is apparent that, in order to function, a religiously pluralistic democracy will require that the ruling majority, the government, be prevented from enshrining religious belief or practice into law. Under such rules, religiously neutral, secular law must represent the ultimate temporal authority.

Is Turkey a religiously neutral nation where it is up to the individual to practice religion or not? Certainly not! Compulsory teaching of something euphemistically called lessons of ethics that in reality is a course about Sunni Islam with a few tidbits of other religions added toward the end in order to placate the commissars of the EU is not the portrait of religious-neutral society. It would suffice to ask any Alawite or atheist parent how they view the compulsory religious education offered to their seven-or eight-year-old child.

Furthermore, evidence of a creeping Islamization of the public space is visible everywhere. In some restaurants where foreigners are free to order alcohol, Turkish citizens are denied at the same table. High-level public servants are, most of the time, male graduates of religious high schools—*Imam Hatip*—and their wives would wear the headscarf and cover themselves from head to toe in a long skirt and sleeves. The facial hair is de rigueur, and membership in one of many religious orders/brotherhoods is expected. During the holy month of Ramadan, it is very questionable to find, during noon hours, open diners and restaurants in most of Anatolia's towns and cities. And when they are open, it is unlikely that the restaurants will be serving alcohol.

Even in the local offices of the government administration, the lunchrooms no longer serve food during Ramadan. It is assumed that all workers are observing the religious fast. Elsewhere, appointments to school principal and deputy principal positions mostly go to persons affiliated with the prime minister's party or with any one of several religious orders.

Islam in Turkey may be moderate, but Turkey is definitely not a religious-neutral society. So why would the international media continue to wring their hands and contort their reasoning trying to paint a rosy picture of something that definitely is not? Why are they hell-bent on defining secularist Turks as members of the elite and the Islamists as working-class Anatolians?

> From its beginnings in the 1940s, a powerful chain of bureaucrats, judges and army generals from the secular upper classes has controlled the most important Turkish affairs, while the elected government, currently the Justice and Development Party of Mr. Erdogan, manages more mundane aspects, much like a municipality.[11]

It is remarkable how in a single paragraph the writer could manage to reveal so much of her ignorance regarding the history of the republic. The sons and daughters of the Turkish upper classes have rarely occupied the higher offices of the judiciary and most certainly not of the army. Furthermore, ever since the end of the Second World War and the introduction of multiparty regime in 1950, the secular forces have never achieved absolute majority in any of the successive elections. The names of the premiers that lead their parties to overwhelming majorities could read as the who's who of conservative Muslim majority: Adnan Menderes (1950-61), Süleyman Demirel (1965-71, 1974-78, 1979-80), Turgut Özal (1983-89), Süleyman Demirel (1991-93), Tansu Çiller (1993-96), Necmeddin Erbakan (1997-99), Abdullah Gül (2002-03), Recep Tayyip Erdoğan (2003-   ). You might even add to this list the name of the 1980 coup leader who was an avid proponent of the Turk-Islam synthesis. The first president to visit Mecca for the pilgrimage, he was the architect of the present constitution that made compulsory the teaching of Islam in schools. Several of the above premiers were strong adherents of the Naqshibendi order of Islam. Others were reputed to be adherents of the Kadiriye order. What is just as remarkable is the fact that most of these leaders hailed from the Anatolian hinterland and belonged to families with incomes modest enough to barely qualify them as middle-class. They were definitely not part of the Turkish "elites," a term the Western media in general seem to be so enamored with.

For various reasons, the Western media and, in particular, the liberal Western media are determined to make common cause with the Islamist movement in Turkey. Some are convinced that the Islamist regime is a strong proponent of free market economy and will always do the bidding of multinational corporations and thus serve and protect their financial and economic interests. Others are uneasy about the emergence of nationalist parties, whom they are quick to tag as fascistic. Finally, any party that appears to reflect too closely the sentiments of the Turkish military is considered suspect.

In another of her arrogant and disparaging articles, the *New York Times* reporter Sabrina Tavernise could not come up with any better description of who the architect of modern Turkey was than to refer to Kemal Atatürk as a "former army general."[12]

Fortunately, not every *New York Times* reporter was unaware of who Atatürk was. Steven Kinzer, in his national bestseller *All the Shah's Men,* describes Atatürk's encounter with Reza Shah of Iran:

> In 1934 Reza Shah traveled to Turkey to meet Atatürk. The two men got along famously, but as they toured the Turkish countryside, the Shah became depressed and frustrated as he realized how quickly Turkey was progressing toward modernity and secularism.[13]

Ten years ago, Western media would refer to Islamists as a fringe movement and to the rest as pro-European free marketeers. Nowadays, the Islamist AKP and its leader, Recep Tayyip Erdoğan, are the toast of the international and, especially, European media: "The only Muslim democracy in the Middle East." "The best role model for Islamic regimes in the Middle East." "A promising democracy in the midst of autocratic Arab regimes." And yet such an infatuation is hard to fathom.

In *"Forces of Fortune"* Vali Nasr presented Turkey's "shopping mall culture" as Islam's best version for a "new and improved" Middle East; the antidote against the fundamentalist vision of Islam. But, unfortunately, widespread corruption, a semi literate under-educated middle class, an army of unemployed youth and a working class destroyed by synchophantic political and media elite are no antidotes but rather the main highways leading to fascism and totalitarianism.

So what seems to be the problem? Could it be that they are sufficiently ignorant to distinguish between the genuine article, i.e., a functioning liberal democracy and a fake? And yet it is so simple. Here is an illustration that should make it crystal clear to all. Consider the following: someone living in Illinois' Twelfth Congressional District would go—every other year, during the month of March—to a local polling place to vote during a primary for the man or woman he or she wishes to be Illinois' representative in Congress. Likewise, every sixth year, they would vote for a candidate whom they wish to place on the ballot for the U.S. Senate.

However, had Illinois adopted the rules governing elections in Turkey, the candidates representing each party would have been designated by the titular heads of the Democrat and Republican parties, respectively. There would be no primaries; and therefore, in order to be on the ballot, Senator Dick Durbin and Representative Jerry Costello would have to get the green light from Barack Obama. That would be some democracy! And yet many bleeding heart liberals (the *Economist*, the *New York Times*, the *Washington Post, Le Monde*) and other internationalist conservatives (*Le Figaro, Frankfurter Allgemeine*) are ignoring the creeping fascism and the unbridled greed and corruption under the Islamist rule and are regularly lionizing the Turkish prime minister R. T. Erdoğan and his cronies as the "Democrats on the Bosporus" while at the same time they make a business of trashing the Turkish Armed Forces as an obstacle to their hidden agenda (we will visit that issue later).

But the naked truth is that under the rules governing the Turkish elections, the parliament is filled with the appointed puppets of the party leaders. They owe their allegiances to the leader, and at the first sign of independence, chances are, their names will not be on the ballot at the next election. Is it realistic, therefore, to expect from such a docile legislative body any sort of an attempt to remove the parliamentary immunity of their party leaders, who are accused of all sorts of criminality, corruption, and misdeeds, especially when almost a third of the same parliament are facing similar charges?

The question about how democratic the Turkish regime is can now be answered. The late Ahmet Taner Kışlalı, a Kemalist intellectual who on October 1999 fell victim of a terrorist attack, addressed the issue quite bluntly:

> If democrat are those who are engaged in the politics and selling of religion, then I am not a democrat! . . .

> . . . If democracy is the name of the system which protects the liars, the thieves and all those on the payroll of the ennemies of Turkey, then I am not a democrat! . . .

> . . . If democrat are those who are sapping the foundations of the Republic, then I am not a democrat! . . .

> And I do not wish to be a democrat where such men are called democrat . . . because I am ashamed of sharing with them the same badge.[14]

2

Islamist Agenda

During the past eight years, we have witnessed the evolutionary transformation of Turkey from a secular, nationalist, and Western-oriented country with a thriving free press to a radical, dogmatic, Pan-Islamic, and semiauthoritarian land with a muzzled press. Recently, we have observed a massive hostility toward Israel and open-arm friendship toward the likes of Iran, Syria, Hamas, and even Sudan. Most of the Western media watched with wide eyes Turkish government ministers—eleven of them!—descend on Syria to sign numerous cooperation agreements and announce the removal of visa requirements for travel between Syria and Turkey. A few days later, Erdoğan, while visiting Teheran, declared that Ahmadinejad was a good and trustworthy friend of Turkey and that Iran had every right to develop nuclear power. Given the fact that there were other Middle Eastern countries with nuclear weapons (Israel?), he suggested that the debate over the banning of nuclear weapons should include their weapons too.

Which brings us to the following question: why should anyone be surprised by the foreign policy thrust of this Islamist government? Turkey had another Islamist government a decade or so ago. And the result was not too different.

> Scenes that unfolded in this working-class suburb of Ankara over the last few days have stunned millions of Turks who want to believe that their country, even though it is now governed by an Islamist Prime Minister, will remain a secular democracy.

> On one recent evening, several hundred people jammed a hall in Sincan to celebrate "Jerusalem Day," a holiday proclaimed 17 years ago by Ayatollah Ruhollah Khomeini of Iran. Their host was the local Mayor, and the evening's guest of honor was the Iranian Ambassador, Muhammed Reza Bagheri.

> When Mr. Bagheri arrived, the crowd erupted with chants of "Down with Israel! Down with Arafat!" He then stepped to the podium and delivered a fiery speech demanding that Muslims obey the Sharia, the law of the Koran.

"On behalf of Muslims all over the world, I say that we can wait no longer," the Ambassador declared. "Do not be afraid to call yourselves fundamentalists. Fundamentalists are those who follow the words and actions of the Prophet. God promised them the final victory."[15]

The Education Jihad

Until lately, Western officials and media routinely applauded every move undertaken by Turkey's Islamist regime as revolutionizing the internal politics or as another step in the direction of Turkey's accession into the European Union. Always uppermost in their mind has been the absolute devotion of the Justice and Development Party (AKP) to a free market economy. However, for those who watched AKP's Islamization policy rather closely, the real story lay elsewhere.

The ruling majority and the Erdoğan government pursued the dismantling of the Kemalist infrastructure of the republic with a four-prong attack. Of these, the most insidious and the most reprehensible one involved the educational system. Not that the attacks on the judiciary, the independent media, and the empowerment of a crony capitalism producing religious oligarchs by the thousands and feeding a culture of corruption could be easily ignored.

But the real danger to the secular Turkish Republic is in the systematic dismantling, by the AKP, of Turkey's state-run unitary educational system. The prime minister has repeatedly ignored admonitions from the courts and pursued a deliberate policy to erode the distinction between religious and public education. In the process, Turkey has now thousands of Imam-Hatip schools and about four or five thousand more official state-run Qur'an courses, not counting the unofficial Qur'an schools, which may bring the total number to about forty thousand. All schools are delivering the same Sunni version of Islam with a total disregard for the sensitivities of religious minorities such as the Alawites (comprising almost 25 to 30 percent of the nation) and that of the Shiites and many other Muslim sects and minorities. A great number of these religious schools are under the direction of a well-financed religious order and its leader, Fethullah Gülen. The Gülen movement controls a vast media empire, numerous financial institutions and banks, business organizations, an international network of thousands of schools, universities, student residences, and many associations and foundations. It is estimated that his organization controls an unregulated budget of about $30 billion. How much of that is U.S. taxpayer monies disbursed via the CIA is an open question.

Although Fethullah Gülen's religious movement has successfully infiltrated various levels of government and especially the security apparatus, it must be said that there are other quite large and significant religious orders and brotherhoods whose adherents are currently occupying top cabinet posts and are very prominently represented among the new hires in the civil service and, in particular, among the teachers of state-run elementary and high schools.

Naqshibendi Republic of Turkey

In order to better grasp the significance of the Islamist takeover of Turkey's governance, a brief historic look at the role of various Islamic religious orders have played in the past in various corners of the Muslim world is useful.

- The French push to colonize North Africa has been quite effectively aided by the collaboration between a Muslim brotherhood (Tariqat Tijaniyya), mostly to be found in North and West Africa, and the French army.
- A similar collaboration between the British colonial administration in India and another Muslim brotherhood (Ahmadiyya) eased the colonization of Muslim India by the British Empire.
- In a far more bloody encounter in the Arabian Desert, the British—in collaboration with the followers of Salafi Islam (a stricter version of Wahhabi Islam), the forces of the ruler of Mecca and Medina Emir Hussein and the Berber tribes—routed and killed nearly a quarter of a million Turkish solders. The end result of which was the colonization of Saudi Arabia.
- The end of the First World War saw the British at it once again, this time enlisting the help of the Qadiriyya order along with the followers of the Naqshibendi brotherhood before invading and capturing Kerkuk, Mosul, and Mesopotamia and eventually colonizing Iraq and Jordan.
- Even after the birth in 1923 of the Turkish Republic, the British continued to push the Islamic button on several other occasions: in 1924, the Nasturi rebellion, and the following year, the Naqshibendi—better known as the Sheikh Said—rebellion were directed against a Muslim nation.

For religious orders and brotherhoods, collaboration with the infidel is admissible so long as the price is right. And for the Ahmadis, the Salafis, the Qadiris, or the Naqshibendis of this world, the essential question has always been whether the French or the British treasuries were reliable paymasters.

Mustafa Kemal Atatürk viewed such religious orders as an existential threat against the young republic, enemies who would not hesitate one second before collaborating with the enemies of Turkey. And now the republic he founded from the ashes of a defunct Ottoman Empire is in bed with the like of Wahhabis of Saudi Arabia, and the Hamas and Hezbollah of the Middle East.

So the central question one should ask is, where does Islam fit in the building of an open society? Under Islam, can one expect tolerance of people you don't agree with? The Turkish National Security Council, in a communiqué it issued during the previous Islamist government, had reminded that in Turkey, "secularism is not only a form of government but a way of life and the guarantee of democracy and social peace." It remains to be seen if those words are still valid under the present Islamist regime. Looking at the present political and social landscape of Turkey, one would have to admit that those words ring hollow. On the contrary, today, the Kemalist republic is looking more and more like the Naqshibendi Republic of Turkey.

Rule of Law—Alla Turca

Separation of powers—between the executive, the legislative, and the judiciary—is a sine qua non condition for a properly functioning democracy. When Prime Minister (PM) Erdoğan rammed through the parliament a bill aimed at lowering the mandatory retirement age of judges, he has, in effect, forcibly retired several thousand secular judges who questioned AKP's interpretation of the constitution. Moreover, when he moved to replace them with his cronies and with judges displaying solid and visible religious credentials, such as facial hair and a wife wearing a headscarf, the message to the secular establishment was loud and clear. Evidently, it was not loud enough to register with the Western governments and media and, in particular, with the European Union.

The PM's attitude toward the European Court of Human Rights (ECHR) is another prime example of his contempt for international as well as national court decisions that are not in agreement with his Islamization policies. Indeed, when the ECHR upheld the Turkish Constitutional Court's decision against permitting headscarves in Turkish universities, he declared that only Islamic religious scholars—ulema—could issue such a judgment. What made the prime minister furious about the court's decision was the fact that the ECHR held that there had been no violation of

   i.   Article 9 of the European Convention on Human Rights regarding the freedom of thought, conscience, and religion;
  ii.   Article 2 of Protocol No. 1 regarding the right to education;
 iii.   Article 8 regarding the right to respect for private and family life;
 iv.   Article 10 regarding the freedom of expression; and
  v.   Article 14 regarding the prohibition of discrimination.

In its decision, the court elaborated about the notion of secularism and found it to be consistent with the value underpinning the European Convention on Human Rights. It affirmed that upholding that principle was necessary to protect the democratic system in Turkey. The court recognized that the prohibition of wearing the Islamic headscarf in universities was based, in particular, on the principles of secularism and equality. Indeed, the Turkish Constitutional Court, in its decision, had declared the principle of secularism as the guarantor of democratic values and the meeting point of liberty and equality. The principle prevented the state from manifesting a preference for a particular religion of belief. It entailed freedom of religion and conscience. It also served to protect the individual not only against arbitrary interference by the state but also from external pressure of extremist movements. Furthermore, the court noted that the freedom to manifest one's religion could be restricted in order to defend those values and principles.

The ECHR viewed the issue from another angle too. It noted the emphasis placed in the Turkish constitutional system on the protection of the rights of women. Gender equality—recognized by the European court as one of the key principles underlying the convention and a goal to be achieved by member states of the Council of Europe—had also been found by the Turkish Constitutional Court to be a principle implicit in the values underlying the constitution.

In addition, like the Turkish court, the ECHR considered that, when examining the question of the Islamic headscarf in the Turkish context, it had to be borne in mind the impact that wearing such a symbol, which was presented or perceived as a compulsory religious duty, may have on those who chose not to wear it. The issues at stake included the protection of the "rights and freedoms of others" and the "maintenance of public order" in a country in which the majority of the population, while professing a strong attachment to the rights of women and a secular way of life, adhered to the Islamic faith. Imposing limitations on the freedom to wear the headscarf could, therefore, be regarded as meeting a pressing social need by seeking to achieve those two legitimate aims, especially since that religious symbol had taken on political significance in Turkey in recent years.

The European Court of Human Rights did not lose sight of the fact that there were extremist political movements in Turkey that sought to impose on society as a whole their religious symbols and conception of a society founded on religious precepts.

Against that background, the court concluded that

> it was the principle of secularism which was the paramount
> consideration underlying the ban on the wearing of religious symbols

in universities. In such a context, where the values of pluralism, respect for the rights of others and, in particular, equality before the law of men and women were being taught and applied in practice, it was understandable that the relevant authorities should consider it contrary to such values to allow religious attire, including, as is the case before the Court, the Islamic headscarf, to be worn on University premises.[16]

It would be misleading to assume that with the headscarf issue thus settled, the matter of disrespect for the rule of law has now been put to rest. There are just as serious and just as ominous developments throughout the land. Unfortunately, official circles in the West are nearly oblivious to these negative reports.

One controversy began with a German prosecutor's indictment of a German-based charity active among the country's Turkish community. Among the charges was one that stated that the German-based charity Lighthouse e. V. president, M. Gürhan; Turkish Channel 7 owner, Z. Karaman; and Turkey's Supreme Board of Radio and Television president, Z. Akman (he no longer serves as president) were complicit in channeling charity money to Turkey and disbursing it for causes other than those claimed by the charity. Charity directors Gürhan, M. Taşkan, and F. Ermiş were arrested in a police raid into the charity and company buildings. They testified that most of the money (€41.3 million) was sent to Turkey by couriers, an illegal act under German law. Akman, barred entry into Germany until 2012, is accused of being a courier between Lighthouse e. V. and Turkish Islamist Channel 7.

Some additional rumors circulating and reported in some newspapers alleged that Erdoğan's son may have been one of the couriers. Other newspapers reported a portion of the German prosecutor's indictment. The indictment suggested that "attempts were made by the Turkish government to apply political pressure, in order to secure the release of the suspects from prison." Moreover, the indictment included an unsigned receipt indicating that an unspecified amount of money was forwarded to the Turkish prime minister for delivery to tsunami victims in Southeast Asia. There is no evidence that such a disaster relief fund has ever been sent to Indonesia. According to the indictment, there is a witness testimony verifying this version of events.

When Doğan Media Group newspapers began publishing the above allegations of corruption, it became the target of tax-evasion charges and investigations. Over thirty tax inspectors descended on the group's central offices for over a year, combing through its books. The result was a crippling $3.2 billion demand in fines and penalties.

Speaking to a reporter for the *Wall Street Journal* in Istanbul, the Turkish media mogul Aydın Doğan accused the prime minister of seeking to muzzle criticism and create a "calm and silent Turkey."[17] He added that "the basis for all this is political." During the same interview, Mr. Doğan said that seven of the prime minister's companies were being investigated by tax inspectors. Relations with the government, he said, first "went haywire" early last year when his media outlets reported on the business dealings of Mr. Erdoğan's son and the wife of another son. The mood soured further when Mr. Doğan's newspapers started digging into a criminal case in Germany involving a Turkish charity accused of funneling funds to Mr. Erdoğan's AK Party. "Mr. Erdoğan came to power using democracy. He is a product of democracy, but he can accept democracy only for himself. He cannot accept side components of democracy such as free media."

Judicial concerns have been expressed also in a case known as Ergenekon, a criminal investigation that has led to the arrests of over two hundred individuals suspected of being members of a murky, extralegal organization that is suspected of having close ties to the military and the bureaucracy. In a paper for the Central Asia-Caucasus Institute Silk Road Studies Program at John Hopkins University's Paul H. Nitze School for Advanced International Studies, Gareth Jenkins has analyzed in great detail the good and the ugly aspects of the criminal investigations, raising serious judicial concerns about the integrity of the whole affair.[18] His judicial concerns include the manner in which the investigation as a whole has been handled, the disregard for due process, the prosecutors' inability or unwillingness to understand the numerous contradictions in the indictments, the creative interpretation and occasional apparent manipulation of what little evidence is adduced, the arbitrary nature of many of the police raids, the length of time some of the suspects have been detained in prison without being formally charged, the frequency with which materials related to the case or its critics have been leaked into the public domain, and the subsequent suspicion that the investigation has become tainted by political motives. In conclusion, he raised the alarm:

> Even the most cursory objective examination of the investigation raises deeply disturbing questions, which multiply and intensify the more closely the alleged evidence in the case is examined.

There is another sordid aspect of this affair. Most of the monitored and recorded telephone conversations appended to the dossiers—each file over two thousand pages thick—involve critics and opponents of the AKP. In most cases, their conversations are published in pro-AKP media outlets and Web sites. And yet under Turkish law, tapping a telephone conversation without judicial approval is a crime, as is publishing the transcript of a wiretap. In the opinion of Gareth Jenkins,

[Ergenekon] represents a major step not—as its proponents maintain—towards the consolidation of pluralistic democracy in Turkey, but towards an authoritarian one-party state.[19]

What is remarkable about all this is the fact that the West has been curiously quiet about these shameless assaults on the rule of law. Once the democratic "model" for the Muslim world, Turkey nowadays looks more like a semiauthoritarian regime where the "cult of the personality" has been enshrined, the media muzzled, and the corrupt are ruling with impunity.

The irony of it is that some illegal recordings of the prime minister's conversations with some of his wealthy friends also began to surface. They present the profile of a politician asking his businessman friend to wire $25,000 to his daughter who, at the time, was studying at Indiana University in the USA.

Finally, there is also the case of a judge who must have been working overtime approving wiretaps, right and left, that he ended up ordering the police to listen to him too! Yes, it was revealed that the judge who approved the tapping of phone conversations of some forty-four people had authorized a list containing his own telephone number too! A columnist for the daily *Hürriyet* concluded,

> The Republic of Turkey is rapidly going down into a "precipice
> of distrust." No one trusts anyone. Distrust is rampant among the
> various institutions of the Republic.[20]

Pravda—Alla Turca

In its latest worldwide ranking of free media, for the year 2009, the Paris-based international nongovernmental organization Reporters Sans Frontiere (RSF) has placed Turkey 122nd out of 175 countries. Turkey last year ranked 102nd. This indicates a slippage of 20, placing her in the bottom one-third for press freedom. According to the leading press watchdog, Turkey is performing worse with each passing year. This year's poor showing, according to RSF, is due to a surge in cases of censorship, especially censorship of media that represent minorities (above all Kurdish publications) and effort by members of government bodies to maintain their control over coverage of matters of general interest.

Another significant factor has been the attempt by the government to mute the voice of the opposition by resorting to escalated verbal attacks and applying crippling tax fines. There are some similarities between the intimidation methods and outright takeovers of unfriendly media outlets adopted by the ruling AKP in Turkey and the tactics used to muzzle the opposition in Russia by Prime Minister Putin.[21] In fact, the takeover two years ago of Turkey's second-largest daily, *Sabah*, by the state-owned Savings and Deposit Insurance Fund is a classic case that prompted several observers to compare it to that undertaken by Putin in Russia against Media-Most. *Sabah* was subsequently sold by the state-run agency to a company where the PM's son-in-law became CEO. Even though one can look at this case from a press freedom point of view, nepotism is an issue too. But when it became known that the buyer had secured credit from two state banks, the issue became one of corruption at the highest levels of government. Furthermore, the question as to what collateral was offered to secure such a large credit is still shrouded in mystery.

According to the *Wall Street Journal*,

> language directly attacking the prime minister and stories about his immediate family are off-limits. Editors in secular media outlets think twice before running a story criticizing the government for introducing Islam into Turkey's strictly secular public domain.[22]

The *Journal* reports that top editors and media tycoons complain of widespread wiretaps. Even cartoonists have been sued, with Erdoğan forcing an independent comic paper, the *Penguen*, to pay compensation for depicting him as various animals.

On the other hand, any student of the AKP would concede that the Islamist regime gives top priority to efforts aimed at manipulating the public opinion. The ruling party's "public relations" policies are, without any doubt, far more effective than that of any other national party past and/or present. AKP pays great importance to public surveys it conducts and has used its friendly media to orchestrate the dissemination of misinformation with the ultimate goal of solidifying the present oligarchic order. Even though the takeover of *Sabah* and ATV media group had given AKP a prominent voice in both print and electronic media, the regime has many more lackeys who are vying for the rewards that usually follow such partisan activities. In fact, no other ruling majority in the past has tried as hard as AKP to establish a partisan media supported and funded by Islamist capital.

One such media group, Zaman, is owned and controlled by the Fethullah Gülen brotherhood. It serves mostly the radical Islamist wing of the party. It is distributed free of charge at different locations and benefits mainly from the announcements and public notices placed by local municipalities and by government ministries. The paper's circulation numbers are obviously misleading, and they do not give any indication as to the breadth of its appeal.

Another media group (Albayraklar) closely associated with the Islamist regime controls *Yeni □afak* newspaper and TVNET. It too appeals to the religious right and is actively engaged in promoting the Islamist agenda. The Albayraklar group's relationship with Erdoğan dates way back to the days when Erdoğan was mayor of Istanbul. Then a relatively obscure travel and tourism company, Albayraklar became the main beneficiary of large-city contracts during Erdoğan's tenure as mayor, securing several large refuse-collection contracts as well as a very controversial bid for part of the Istanbul Subway construction. In fact, Erdoğan's first initiative as mayor had been to cancel a subway contract won by Siemens and later award it to Albayraklar Group. At the time, the German reaction to Erdoğan's snub of Siemens came through Karl Nuebeck, the transportation director of Siemens, who was accompanying the German foreign minister Klaus Kinkel in Istanbul. Nuebeck had declared that Erdoğan canceled the deal in order to give it to his friends. It was the first of many shady deals consummated, over the years, between Erdoğan and Albayraklar.

Another example of a businessman hitching his wagon to the Islamist regime and beginning to feed from the trough and eventually becoming a partisan media mogul is Ethem Sancak. An influential member of the Association of Turkish Businessmen and Industrialists, an elite group of industrialists and businessmen with an inordinate influence in the affairs of the nation, his newspaper, *Star*, and Kanal 24 television station joined the chorus of Erdoğan sympathizers. In fact, he declared that Erdoğan was his "idol!"

The Islamist regime's determination to control the print and electronic media throughout the country is about to be complete. The Doğan Media Group is the last remaining significant media group that is not controlled by a business group close to AKP government. Halil M. Karaveli, managing editor of *Turkey Analyst*, states,

> After having accused the Kemalist state of imposing a particular order on society, Islamic conservatism has embarked on its own version of social engineering, employing state power in order to mold the realm of the media in its own vision. Indeed, the determination

of the AKP government to create a subservient media cannot but kindle the suspicion that the long-term goal is to mold society along Islamic conservative lines.[23]

Erdoğan and the Radical Islamist Camp

Prime Minister Erdoğan takes great pride in his cochairmanship, along with the Spanish premier Jose Luis Rodriguez Zapatero, of the Alliance for Civilization, a UN-sponsored affair that reflects mostly the views of the Organisation of the Islamic Conference (OIC). Although the present secretary-general of the conference is a Turkish citizen, the Muslim brotherhood has become a driving force within the conference. At its 1990 Cairo meeting, OIC has issued a Declaration on Human Rights in Islam. It concludes with the caveat that "all the rights and freedoms stipulated in this Declaration are subject to the Islamic Shariah." For a secular state (Turkey) to opt for the Shariah rather than the UN's Universal Declaration of Human Rights says a lot about the priorities of its leaders.

The reality is that Erdoğan's Turkey has moved incrementally and inexorably toward the radical Islamist camp of Iran, Syria, Hezbollah, and Hamas. And he was rewarded for his devotion to the Islamist cause by being the recipient of the 2009 King Abdullah II Award for Excellence in Good Government and Transparency!

But the Western governments have continued to make excuses for the new Turkish policy move. Indeed, AKP owes a great deal of gratitude to the Western powers for its ability to consolidate its control over just about every organ of governance in Turkey as well as what was once a thriving free press. Here is how one observer viewed the Western attitude toward Turkey:

> The Bush administration ignored the warnings of secular Turkish leaders in country's media, military and diplomatic corps that Erdoğan was a wolf in sheep's clothing. Rather than pay attention to his past attempts to undermine Turkey's secular, pro-Western character and treat him with a modicum of suspicion, after the AKP electoral victory in 2002 the Bush administration upheld the AKP and Erdoğan as paragons of Islamist moderation and proof positive that the US and the West have no problem with political Islam. Erdoğan's softly peddled but remorselessly consolidated Islamism was embraced by senior American officials intent on reducing democracy to a synonym for elections rather than acknowledging that democracy is only meaningful as a system of laws and practices that engender liberal egalitarianism.[24]

Of course, none of that could dull the enthusiasm of some Western pundits, scholars, and analysts to laud the Islamist leaders in terms approaching those that were reserved, a few years back, for the leaders operating behind a certain iron curtain.

> In the course of three short generations, Turkey has developed a **vibrant, exciting,** and **responsive democracy** that is now dominated by a **competent political party,** with a decided Islamic personality.[25]

Yes, a democracy for the oligarchs, for those engaged in widespread corruption. Yes, a democracy for those cheating the treasury through the sale or purchase of state property. A democracy at the service of miscreants, of embezzlers, and of those engaged in laundering money.

Graham Fuller, former head of the CIA's Middle East-Turkey desk, is a name quite familiar to the Turkish media. At the height of the bloody Kurdish uprising, he was reported to have advocated autonomy for the Kurds living in the southeastern Turkey and, in later years, became an ardent advocate of the so-called Turk-Islam synthesis and a regular contributor to Fethullah Gülen movement's Abant Forum. Through these annual roundtables, the movement has managed to reach a wide sector of the Western establishment and to dispel any fear that the Gülen movement might seek to impose an Islamic or Shariah state. How much of the views he advocates represent unofficial positions of the United States administration is hard to know. However, Fuller's views have received great attention in the Islamist media in Turkey and have earned him a reputation as the deep voice of the United States diplomatic establishment. To many, in Turkey, he is the behind-the-scenes architect of the so-called moderate Islam in the Middle East.

> [I]t is remarkable that in Turkey today such crucial theoretical and ideological discussions—about Islam, secularism, Islamist evolution, the view of the past, modern values, and relations with the Muslim world—are discussed and debated more widely by Islamists than any other political or social group.
>
> . . . At this point, the Islamists represent—even by default—the most creative intellectual force in the country on these conceptual questions.

. . . The joint phenomena of the JDP (the Justice and
Development Party known by its Turkish acronym AKP-ss) and
the Gülen movement are emblematic of this fact and demonstrate
the emergence of a creative and vibrant Islamist community within
Turkey.[26]

Graham Fuller's praise for the intellectual capacity of the Islamist
movement is only matched by his vitriolic attacks on the Kemalist movement.
For Fuller Kemal, Atatürk's policy decision to turn toward the West and ignore
the Middle East was a historic error, which he called the "Kemalist historical
lobotomy."

Atatürk, Yes; Kemalism, No

The Kemalist institutions established by the republic (including and
especially the Turkish Armed Forces) have never been the favorites of Turkish
Islamists—the Naqshibendis, the Fethullah brotherhood, the promoters of the
New Republic or the Second Republic, the old leftists who switched sides to
become the neoliberals funded by George Soros. However, among other critics
of Kemalism, especially among some writers and Islamist scholars, the cool
approach has always been to distinguish between the Kemalism of the Atatürk
era and the Kemalism of post-Atatürk period. Recently, Nobel laureate Orhan
Pamuk—who, ever since establishing residence in New York City and lecturing
at Columbia, has become a regular of the *Charlie Rose Show*—has added his
pedigree to the above list of the enemies of the secular Republicans. According
to Pamuk, "Atatürk's secularism was the right one," but "the secularists of
today do not have much respect for human rights."[27] In short, yes to Atatürk
and no to Kemalism, as if the two were not the two sides of the same coin.

It needs to be said that all Turkish institutions were established by, and
thus belong to, the republic. Furthermore, Kemalism has been the founding
ideology of the republic. But it did not emerge from a manifesto or a public
declaration of principles and intentions leading to a revolution. It evolved as
a form of user's guide to help in the progress of the republic. As such, it was
never meant to be a compilation of reactionary principles. On the contrary,
it still represents a series of reforms geared to prepare a feudal, illiterate,
and dirt-poor nation to rise, in the words of its great leader, "to the level of
contemporary civilization."

The Islamist scholar Hakan Yavuz follows the line of many other neosecularists and sees a conflict between democracy and Kemalism.

> But the history of modern Turkey is the story of conflict between democracy and Kemalism. Democracy brought people to the public space, but their identity claims have been perceived as a threat for the Kemalist system and the army regularly has intervened to eliminate these identity claims and close off opportunity space.

> In Turkey the Islamic movements have been neither anti-modern nor backward. Rather they are identity and justice-seeking movements. Such movements seek to reclaim the Muslim "self," which is perceived as being robbed of its authenticity and identity.[28]

If you cut the jargon out of this narrative, you will realize that what for the author is "identity claim" is in fact a claim for the primacy of Islam over what the Kemalist republic assiduously tried to build: a "nation," the primacy of an identity as member of the *umma* as opposed to that of a citizen of the Turkish nation; and there can be no meeting of the minds on such a fundamental issue. Make no mistake: those who find Kemalism abhorrent are also critical of Atatürk as an enemy of Islam. But the core issue remains: Mustafa Kemal saved an 80 percent illiterate nation from ruin and misery and gave it all the tools essential for developing as a modern society. Let me put it as bluntly as possible: the prevailing conditions around 1923 were not conducive to asking for the vote of the people in order to remove the sultan, to end the caliphate, and to adopt a republican form of government. So the claim that the history of Turkey is the story of conflict between democracy and Kemalism is just a risible one.

The intriguing question has always been, what makes the sight of a moderately Islamic Turkey that has finally gotten rid of its Kemalist past so pleasing to Western eyes?

Could it be the vision of a neo-Ottoman regime just as corrupt and bankrupt as its predecessor, waiting hat in hand—since forty-plus years—to be invited to enter into the bosom of Europa? Yet it was all those leaders whose reference has always been Islam—Menderes, Demirel, Evren, Özal, Erbakan, Gül, and Erdoğan—that bastardized Atatürk's understanding of secularism, nationalism, republicanism, and reformism and turned over the republic to the architects of the Turk-Islam synthesis.

Objectivity, in the course of analyzing the Islamist movement's the past few decades, would quickly belie the contention that this was a movement that was denied its "identity." Indeed, starting with former prime minister Erbakan's ideology—expressed through his political movement, National Order/Millî Nizam, and the successive parties he founded (National Salvation/Milli Selâmet, Welfare/Refah, Felicity/Saadet, and Virtue/Fazilet)—up to AKP, founded by his old student the current prime minister Erdoğan, we observe that they were all geared to appeal to the conservative base of the Islamist movement. These were parties that excelled in the art of blending populist policies with sectarian politics.

Mahmood Mamdani, in his detailed and most informative book[29] about the Sudan's sectarian religious confrontations, elaborates about the problems facing the country during its struggle for nation and state building. He provides lengthy quotations from an eminent religious intellectual Hassan al-Turabi, who was the head of the National Islamic Front (NIF) of Sudan:

> Muslims have failed to absorb and understand their history. They are not able to renew their movement because they do not understand the ever-changing movement of history. They have assumed that human thought, or the body of achievement of Islamic *ijtihad*, is not connected in any way to time and place . . .

> I am not in favor of sitting somewhere and issuing a fatwa and forcing people to accept it. Nor am I by any means a believer in a church that monopolizes the truth and separates man from God. I regret to say that the Muslims have been affected by the Western malaise, and they have developed pseudo-churches where *"ulema"* and sheikhs pontificate and issue sacred edits . . . Knowledge is a common commodity and people attain various degrees of it, and can exercise *ijtihad* at various levels.

Now some readers, unaware of the authorship of these comments, could easily attribute them to a young Mustafa Kemal admonishing his followers about the threat posed by those who would monopolize the truth. Turabi's comments about the ulema invite comparison with those of Prime Minister Erdoğan, who chastised the European Court of Human Rights for issuing an opinion about headscarf rather than let the ulema decide.

Mahmood Mamdani interprets the above comments as a set of warnings against sectarian Islam, which he accuses of confusing the general principles of the religion with values and practices prevalent in specific places at particular times. Indeed, he paraphrases Turabi's remarks by stating that the practice of Islam in Iran is packaged in "Iranian chauvinism" and that Pakistani version comes bundled with a legacy of the Indian caste system, with total separation of women from men. He quotes Hassan al-Turabi:

> I fear that [*Jama'at-e-Islami* of Pakistan] might have been influenced by some of the traditions of the Indian culture . . . Women are totally separated from men, which of course has nothing to do with Islam, and a religion that is for men only is a deformed religion.

Turabi, who once sponsored the presence of Osama bin Laden in Sudan and was a mentor of Ayman al-Zawahiri, is often referred to as the most significant Muslim cleric since Ayatollah Khomeini. His warning of the need to distinguish Islamic principles from their particular cultural wrapping, which he called Arabism, is quite revealing. That statement too could have been attributed easily to the "former army general."

If one agrees with the proposition that, even today, Turkey is quite a long way from developing the necessary conditions for the proper functioning of a democratic process within the context of a constitutional liberalism, then the argument that Kemalism is an honest attempt to build a viable social infrastructure conducive for such a goal, i.e., democracy, becomes inescapable.

Finally, a most puzzling question: Why is it that all the Western pundits, talking heads, political analysts, and liberal politicians, when analyzing the Islamist regime in Turkey, will touch upon almost anything and everything except the endemic corruption and the criminality? In fact, a few years ago, when the Turkish economy in the Anatolian hinterland wasn't going bust as it is now, referring to Islamist Calvinists and drawing a parallel with the Protestant ethic was a very "cool" idea. And yet a cursory reading of Max Weber should make these commentators think again:

> [T]hat the spirit of hard work, of progress, or whatever else it may be called, the awakening of which one is inclined to ascribe to Protestantism, must not be understood, as there is a tendency to do, as joy of living nor in any other sense as connected with the Enlightenment. The old Protestantism of Luther, Calvin, Knox, Voet, had precious little to do with what today is called progress.[30]

Here is a reminder to all those "see nothing, hear nothing, and say nothing" Western liberal friends (?):

> Atatürk did not rob the people!
> And he did not enrich himself at the expense of the rest of the nation.

3

Multinational State

The Separatist Movement

On October 12, 1915, Theodore Roosevelt declared,

> The one absolutely certain way of bringing [a] nation to ruin, of
> preventing all possibility of its continuing to be a nation at all, would
> be to permit it to become a tangle of squabbling nationalities.[31]

In one of his recent columns, Fatih Altaylı—a well-known journalist who had
his heydays writing for *Hürriyet* then for *Sabah* and now Habertürk—laments
about the level of the public discourse taking place in the Turkish media, noting
that some have succumbed to such hate-filled pronouncements that they have
finally declared Atatürk as fascist. He ventures to predict the approaching end
of the Turkish nation-state:[32]

> If the present trend continues this country will be divided
> within 20 years. At least into two . . . Perhaps into more parts. And
> finally, I take note of the fact that there will be not very many people
> left around who will be sorry to see that happen. Actually all the
> preparations have aimed to achieve that goal. By slowly breaking
> them in, and by slowly wearing them out . . . either someone in
> this country will do it with courage and under control . . . or it will
> happen by violent means. In any case the trend is such that we will
> be spending the remaining few years of our lives and our children
> the bulk of theirs, under totally different circumstances.

Another pointed warning came from Ertuğrul Özkök, former managing
editor of *Hürriyet*. Alluding to the public's violent reaction in Izmir against
Kurdish demonstrators holding posters and signs of the terrorist PKK (Partiya
Karkerên Kurdistan or Kurdistan Workers' Party), he recalls an interview he

had with the interior minister two months earlier during which he warned the AKP minister Beşir Atalay:

> You keep mentioning the risk of South East Anatolia seceding. However, if you fail to manage properly the Kurdish problem, one day you may be surprised to notice that secession signals are beginning to come from the Aegean region.

He went on to remind his readers:

> Indeed, today in a substantial number of citizens living in the Aegean region, the feeling that "they already would have been admitted into the EU, had it not been for the Southeast" is a thought that is taking root.[33]

How did we reach this point? Is the Turkish nation-state doomed?

Let's begin with some historical facts. The Ottoman Empire was the last multiethnic and multireligious empire. Several nations, millet, were cohabitating under the sultan's rule. Nevertheless, the Ottoman power structure relied on the unifying umbrella of Islam. The 1839 and 1878, reforms—Tanzimat—were the hesitant first steps toward a certain form of nationhood. The sultan's subjects were granted equal civil rights without regard for their religious beliefs. And in order to placate the objections of the religious right who saw in these reforms the nefarious hand of the infidel Western powers, the Islamic concept of Ottomanism became the ideology of nationhood. The organizational instrument used by the sultan to achieve the goal of Islamic Ottomanism has been the Naqshibendi order. Although the effort proved to be fruitless, as one Christian component after another of the empire began to peel off, the significance of the Naqshibendi brotherhood's involvement in the affairs of the state was going to have a long-term effect. The Islamic ideology underpinning the empire's cohesion failed to maintain the unity of the state even among its Muslim components. So by the end of the Great War as the empire collapsed, the "state" had shed most of its Christian components—Bulgarians, Serbs, Macedonians, Greeks, Armenians—and, in return, had to absorb almost five million Muslim subjects from Bosnia, Bulgaria, Serbia, Albania, Georgia, and the North Caucasus—Chechens, Abkhaz, Ossetians. As for the Kurds, who were an indigenous group, they remained loyal subjects although, from time to time, religious rebellions flared up only to be suppressed by the armed forces.

A common history, a common language, and a common geographical land are the three essential elements that help assemble the mortar that binds people together and form what we call a nation. In that respect, all of the above people, except for the Kurds, were easily assimilated within the New Republic. Its failure to reach out to the Kurdish regions of southeast Turkey and develop the region's human potential through education and social emancipation—empowerment of women, ending the grip of the feudal lords over the citizenry, developing intolerance to the influence of extremist religious orders and brotherhoods—were the main causes of the underdeveloped region's festering unrest. Indeed, in a report dated December 10, 1936, Celal Bayar, who later served in 1938 as prime minister and in 1950 as president, offers a most succinct and accurate description of the situation:

> eastern provinces, prior to the establishment of the Republic, have never been totally under our control. Previous governments chose to establish their control over the population by securing the services of sheikhs and feudal lords (aga) who, in order to maintain their position among their tribes were turning over to government officials a portion of their loots.[34]

And yet the Turkish Republic, throughout its relatively young history, showed a remarkable degree of ethnic-blind attitude in selecting the nation's leaders. The second president of the republic, Ismet İnönü, longtime associate of Kemal Atatürk, was a Kurd. So too was the reformist president Turgut Özal. Indeed, Hasan Cemal, in his magisterial work—*Kürtler* (The Kurds)—quotes Abdülmelik Fırat:[35]

> A while back the country was in search of a prime minister. The three names under consideration were, all three of them, Kurds: Bülent Ecevit, Ismet Sezgin and Yalım Erez. If you visit in Kastamonu the headstone of Ecevit's grand father you will find out that it reads "Kürtoğlu (son of Kurd) Mustafa Bey." Furthermore, Ismet Sezgin[36] hails from Alevi Kurds who were exiled from Kemah to Aydın.[37]

Hasan Cemal adds,

> Over the ruins of an empire where twenty four different ethnicity, twenty languages, several religions, sects, cultures and nations cohabitated, the only way to reach the contemporary civilization was through becoming a nation and building a nation-state.[38]

Even though old Kurdish rebellions were essentially inspired by religious fanaticism, the present political confrontation is separatist in nature. The Islamist regime's solution to the conflict appears to be a mixture of concessions and old-fashioned religious appeal to unity under Islam. If one considers the preamble to the Turkish constitution, such efforts are doomed; and if pursued to the bitter end, they may lead to charges of treason against those who would be instigating them. Any attempt that might lead to a secession of a part of the republic would be clearly in contradistinction to the constitution.

Indeed, in its preamble, the constitution "affirms the eternal existence of the Turkish nation and motherland and the *indivisible* [emphasis added] unity of the Turkish State" while under Article 3 it states that "the Turkish State, with its territory and nation, is an indivisible entity. Its language is Turkish." But the most ironclad clause, undoubtedly, is Article 4: "The provision of Article 1 of the Constitution establishing the form of the State as a Republic, the provisions in Article 2 on the characteristics of the Republic, and the provision of Article 3 shall not be amended, nor shall their amendment be proposed."[39]

Tangle of Squabbling Nationalities

One could easily conclude that given the parameters of the Turkish constitution, the Kurdish separatism can only lead to a dead end. However, an enlightened leadership of elected Kurdish officials can bridge the gap and meet the aspirations of the Kurds. Here, a couple of critical observations have to be made: First, until and unless southeast Turkey makes progress toward an open society by achieving significant social and cultural changes, a solution to the so-called Kurdish problem will remain a chimera. Only through such social and cultural changes can we expect to move the society from agrarian to industrial and then from industrial to postindustrial levels. At the end of that road, we can expect a progress toward democratization. Second, Turkish electoral law will have to be amended, and the 10 percent threshold requirement for parliamentary representation by a national party will have to be reduced to a reasonable limit of, say, 5 percent. This will enable the Kurdish problem to be debated, not in the mountains by the force of arms, but in parliament with a strong regional party sworn to uphold the constitution and attuned to the interests of its electorate. The present law aims at achieving political and economic stability at the expense of a fair and equitable representation in parliament.

In the meantime, even if the Kurdish cultural heritage continues to shape the citizens' prevailing values, economic and social developments will inevitably bring changes that will shape the future of their society. Economic development in the southeast will bring social and political changes only when it changes people's behavior. Consequently, it will be conducive to democratization to the extent that it creates in the Kurdish areas of the southeast a large, educated, and articulate middle class of people.

Therefore, it is hoped that, as the influence of the separatist movement (PKK) recedes, others will emerge as spokesmen for a Kurdish identity that has explicitly denounced violence while espousing social and economic reforms aimed at dismantling a feudal system that seems to be the root cause of the region's ills.

Unfortunately, the emergence of such a nonviolent, socially progressive, and secular movement will have to overcome the opposition of the PKK, who is not about to relinquish its present undisputed position as the sole representative of the Kurdish people.

In fact, the Fırat News Agency has recently reported that KCK (Koma Ciwaken Kurdistan/Kurdish Communities Union), a front organization of the separatist movement PKK, has issued a seven-point communiqué in which it makes demands that would certainly make any peaceful solution quite difficult. The KCK demands that the road map offered by Abdullah Öcalan be made public; that all military and political operations be stopped immediately; that the constitution be amended and the Kurdish identity be recognized as a component of the nation of Turkey and, as such, be safeguarded and free and equal living conditions be made possible for all to live together; that Kurdish be taught as a language in all schools from primary to university and recognition as their birthright for Kurds to learn, speak, and develop their language and to live in their geography with their historical values, cultures, arts using their mother tongue; that all barriers against Kurdish people's right to organize freely in a democratic society, to engage in politics democratically, and to express itself freely be removed; that all special operation units be withdrawn from the villages, towns, and cities of the region and that the institution of village guards be abolished; and finally, that conditions conducive for the people of the region to develop a secure living environment free from police intimidation be implemented.[40]

The significance of the above road map is not what it says but rather what it omits. Nowhere is there any indication that the terrorist organization is ready to lay down their arms. Note that the communiqué refers to the "people of Turkey" rather than the "Turkish nation." Actually, the PKK was responding to a plan revealed on November 12, 2009, by the Turkish interior minister Beşir Atalay, the coordinator of the government's Kurdish initiative. The plan proposed the following steps:

- Establishment of an independent human rights institution
- Establishment of a commission to oversee antidiscrimination policies
- Parliamentary ratification of the UN Convention against torture

- Establishment of an independent oversight agency to investigate accusations of torture by the security forces
- Renaming of (Kurdish) villages, towns, and cities if so demanded by the locals
- Permission of the use of the Kurdish language during electoral campaigns

It is easy to see that the demands of the PKK are far more extreme and radical than anything the government appears to be ready to offer, although the government had left the door open for future additional moves aimed at meeting some of the Kurdish demands. The major stumbling block is the perception that the government has not developed a well-thought-out plan and is willing to bargain with men who are holding their guns high in the air while professing that they are against any further violence.

The fierce opposition that suddenly developed around the country following the arrival of some thirty PKK members at the Iraqi border and the eagerness with which the government dispatched some local judges to the border in order to process their entry to Turkey was quite revealing. Even though the PKK members refused any offer of amnesty, the government pretended as if they did. Later on, the DTP (Demokratik Toplum Partisi/Democratic Society Party), a pro-PKK national party, had used the group during several road shows where the atmosphere degenerated into real chaos. It's so-called Kurdish Initiative now in tatters; there was no other option for the government but to retreat.

First, with the fiasco at the border still reverberating throughout the land, the government decided to rename its Kurdish Initiative as the new Democratic Initiative. Second, Abdullah Öcalan, the imprisoned founder of the PKK, began to agitate against, what he termed, the harsh prison conditions. This was the excuse to escalate the confrontation between Kurdish and Turkish communities in parts of the country where there were significant numbers of immigrants.

In shantytowns of Istanbul, Kurdish youth took to the streets, tossing Molotov cocktails at buses and cars. In other cities, pro-PKK shop owners closed their shops to support Öcalan. In the southeast of the country, an old enmity raised its ugly head again. Supporters of the Kurdish Hezbullah and the supporters of the PKK exchanged fire and Molotov cocktails. These two groups were responsible for some of the bloodiest confrontations of the 1990s. In Istanbul, the security forces recovered dozens of ready-to-be-used Molotov cocktails and other explosives in the local offices of the DTP. The instructions were to use them against public transports and some grocery chains on the occasion of the foundation of the PKK.

Finally, on December 7, 2009, as the prime minister was entertained at the White House, the news that seven or more soldiers were ambushed in the province of Tokat, in north-central Turkey, had the effect of a cold shower. The ambush may have provided a clear and convincing indication that the PKK is in no mood to support the government's so-called Democratic/Kurdish Initiative. Indeed, the ambush may have changed the whole dynamics of Turkish internal politics.

The cardinal mistake of the Turkish official approach, i.e., the Kurdish Initiative, has been the government's refusal to recognize that the players on the Kurdish side are not just two—the party (DTP) represented in parliament and its armed faction operating from the mountains of northern Iraq, namely the PKK and its current leader, Murat Karayılan. Unfortunately, by now it is becoming painfully clear that anyone ignoring Abdullah Öcalan will have to face the consequences. By proving that he can effectively control the mobs in the urban cities and towns of Turkey, Öcalan has demonstrated that this regime will have to deal with him as the sole representative of the Kurdish people. His reflection on the initiative as being the government's attempt to marginalize the PKK has been the death knell of the current phase of the initiative.

When finally the constitutional court announced its verdict regarding the DTP—closure—no one was too surprised. As it is written, the law had left no choice to the court but to shut down a party that was openly expressing the views and positions of those who had taken arms against the state.

With every passing day, it is becoming apparent that this government has not done its homework, and Turkey is heading toward a point of no return.

In Turkey today, there is no Theodore Roosevelt to warn us of the impending danger. So the answer to the question, "Is Turkey becoming a tangle of squabbling nationalities?" must be a forthright one: if a nation allows itself to be torn apart, it will become a tangle of nationalities. Unfortunately, some segments of the Turkish public are ready and willing to take the low road to perdition. Some greedy intellectuals and the Westernized jet-setting elite and those Islamists who would consider themselves a member of the *umma* rather than a citizen of the secular republic—all these three groups have been, for various reasons, conditioned to feel that expressing pride in a national identity and displaying a real and generous love of country is akin to racism.

Michael Burleigh did address the issue in a most direct way:

> Can a nation-state survive that is only a legal and political shell
> or a "market-state" for discrete ethnic or religious communities that
> share little by way of common values other than the use of the same

currency? Can a society survive that is not the object of commitments to a core values or a focus for the fundamental identities of all its members?[41]

Yet any attempt to seek such a consensus prompts, from the postnational elites enamored with pseudocosmopolitan doctrines of multiculturalism, a reflexive charge of racism. In the words of Seymour Martin Lipset,[42]

> The histories of bilingual and bicultural societies that do not assimilate are histories of turmoil, tension and tragedy.

In today's Turkey, the name of the game is identity politics. More specifically, politics based on Kurdish identity is trying to impose its will upon a regime enslaved to its masters, the Western powers, where it is currently fashionable to predict the demise of nationhood. Strobe Talbott, in an essay he wrote in 1992, predicted it:

> [W]ithin the next hundred years . . . nationhood as we know it will be obsolete; all states will recognize a single, global authority.[43]

The European Union and, particularly some of its member states have, in the past, been a real force for the disunion of Turkey by encouraging, supporting, and financing the PKK. Even when undisputable evidence was indicating the active involvement of the PKK in illegal drug trade throughout Europe, the European countries turned a deaf ear and a blind eye to such activities. As long as PKK was not engaged in terrorist activities on their soil, the issue was of no concern to them.

If one views the present predicament facing Turkey in the Caucasus, in Cyprus, in the Middle East, and in Afghanistan, it is fair to say that Turkish foreign policy will have to navigate some very tortuous waters. Let us look at some of these issues as they occupy a major part of Turkish foreign policy agenda.

The Caucasus and the Armenian-Turkish Conflict

The Armenian-Turkish dossier contains two files. The Armenian demand that Turkey recognizes the historical events surrounding the relocation of the Armenians living in eastern Turkey as a genocide has been the most contentious issue dividing the two parties. The issue of the closing, by Turkey, of the Armenian-Turkish border, following the war between Armenia and Azerbaijan, is a more recent development.

Each year during the month of April, the Armenian lobby in the U.S. Congress pressures the administration to recognize the bloody events that took place between 1915 and 1919 as genocide by passing a resolution. The Armenian National Committee of America (ANCA) and the Armenian Assembly of America (AAA) are among the most powerful lobbies in Congress. Another factor influencing many members of Congress is the fact that Armenian-American communities are largely concentrated in important states such as California, Michigan, and Massachusetts.

There is something peculiar about the way the political class in the United States thinks and operates. For them, this resolution is a great image builder. Although a nonbinding resolution (on the White House and on the State Department), it essentially documents a tragedy that took place nearly one hundred years ago carried out by the Ottoman Empire, which no longer exists. One wonders if a congressional resolution condemning the United States for the Native Indian genocide or another one decrying centuries of slavery will be coming up next.

As for the president, nothing illustrates better the political hypocrisy of the day than the statement of a candidate seeking the votes of single-issue groups as opposed to his statement as president. Indeed, on October 27, 2008, candidate Obama wrote a letter, which read,

> Joe Biden and I believe that the Armenian Genocide is not an allegation, a personal opinion, or a point of view, but rather a widely documented fact supported by an overwhelming body of historical evidence.

But then, on April 6, 2009, speaking at the Grand National Assembly of Turkey, Obama was not speaking of a widely documented fact but of rather differing views:

> I know there's a strong view in this chamber about the terrible events of 1915. And while there's been a good deal of commentary about my views, it's really about how the Turkish and Armenian people deal with the past. And the best way forward for the Turkish and Armenian people is a process that works through the past in a way that is honest, open and constructive.

And what was this "widely documented fact supported by an overwhelming body of evidence"? In a testimony before the U.S. House International Committee, historian Justin McCarty declared,

> Ethnic conflict between Turks and Armenians actually began more than 100 years before World War I. Actions of the Russian Empire precipitated the conflict. In 1800, Armenians were scattered within and beyond a region that now encompasses Armenia, Georgia, Azerbaijan, and Eastern Turkey. In all but small districts, Armenians were a minority which had been under Muslim, primarily Turkish, rule for 700 years. The Russian Empire had begun the imperial conquests of the Muslim lands south of the Caucasus Mountains. One of their main weapons was the transfer of populations and deportation. They ruthlessly expelled whole Muslim populations, replacing them with Christians whom they felt would be loyal to a Christian government. Armenians were a major instrument of this policy. Like other in the Middle East, the primary loyalty of Armenians was religious. Many Armenians resented being under Muslim rule, and they were drawn to a Christian State and to offers of free land (land which had been seized from Turks and other Muslims). A major population exchange began. In Erivan Province (today the Armenian Republic) a Turkish majority was replaced by Armenians. In other regions such as coastal Georgia, Circassia, and the Crimea, other Christian groups were brought in to replace expelled Muslims. There was massive Muslim mortality, in some cases up to one third of the Muslims died.

Professor McCarthy adds,

> The Russians expelled 1.3 million Muslims from 1827 to 1878. One result of this migration, serving the purposes of the Russians, was the development of ethnic hatred and ethnic conflict between Armenians and Muslims.

> Intercommunal war erupted when the Ottoman Empire entered World War I. Armenian revolutionaries, many trained in Russia, attempted to seize many Ottoman cities in Eastern Anatolia. They took the city of Van and held it until Russian invaders arrived, killing all but a few of the Muslims of the city and surrounding villages. In the countryside, Muslim tribesmen killed the Armenians who fell into their hands. Armenian and Kurdish bands killed throughout the

East, and massacre was the rule of the time. Russian and Ottoman regular troops were less murderous, but they too gave little quarter to those viewed as the enemy. Some of the worst civilian deaths of Turks and Armenians came at the end of the war. The killing went on until 1920. Many more died of starvation and disease than from bullets.

The results were among the worst seen in warfare. More than forty percent of the Anatolian Armenians died; similar mortality was the fate of the Muslims of the war zone. In the Province of Van, for example, 60% of the Muslims were lost by the war's end.

Following the occupation of Istanbul at the end of WWI, the British looked everywhere to find evidence in support of Armenian charges that the massacres were an Ottoman government policy. Nothing incriminating could be found among the Ottoman government documents. Similar searches in British archives were fruitless. In failing to find any legally supportable evidence against the Ottoman regime, Lord Curzon, the British foreign secretary at the time, requested Sir A. Geddes, the British ambassador at Washington, "to ascertain if United States Government are in possession of any evidence that could be of value for purpose of prosecution."[44] The British Embassy in Washington returned the following reply: "I regret to inform your Lordship that there was nothing therein which could be used as evidence against the Turks."[45]

There are additional and compelling evidence supporting the above statements. The most convincing belongs to Hovhannes Katchaznouni, the first prime minister of the independent Armenian Republic until August 1919. He was among the founders of the Dashnagtzoutiun Party and one of its top leaders. In a report submitted to the 1923 Party Convention held in Bucharest, Romania, Hovhannes Katchaznouni voiced a self-criticism of the past. The report was published in Armenian and later translated into Russian. An edition of only two thousand copies was published in Tbilisi, Georgia, in 1927. What is interesting but seems natural when the content of the book is taken into consideration is the fact that this historical report by the first Armenian prime minister was banned in Armenia. It is also worth noting that all the copies of the report were collected from libraries throughout Europe by members of the Dashnagtzoutiun. The English edition was first published in 2006.[46] In it, Katchaznouni makes the following observations:

- It was a mistake to establish volunteer units.
- The units were unconditionally allied with the Russian army.

- The decision taken by the Turks to deport the Armenians was an act of self-defense.
- Under Russian tutelage, a Dashnag dictatorship was established in Armenia.
- The Dashnag goal of establishing an Armenia from "sea to sea" provoked, and it was inspired by the imperialist powers.
- Muslim population was subjected to massacres.
- The Armenian terrorist activities were aimed at winning over the Western public opinion.
- The responsibility for the Armenian calamity rested on the shoulders of Dashnagtzoutiun.

In a frank and blunt analysis, Katchaznouni states,

> Again, it would be useless to ask today to what extent the participation of volunteers in the war was a contributory to the Armenian calamity. No one can claim that the savage persecutions would not have taken place if our behavior on this side of the frontier had been different, as no one can claim to the contrary that the persecutions would have been the same even if we had not shown hostility to the Turks.

In a message sent by the Armenian National Bureau to Czar Nicholas II, the Armenian intentions are quite clearly stated:[47]

> As the glorious Russian Armies are fighting against Turkey who, with German support, has dared to raise its hand against mighty Russia, on the land of its own hegemony, in the snowy Armenian mountains and the vast Alashkert valley, the Armenians, taking the advice of their forefathers . . . have risen to sacrifice their lives and their assets to Great Russia and the glory of its throne.

> The Russian flag will freely flutter in the Bosphorus and the Dardanelles.

> You will, my magnificent lord, bestow freedom to the peoples under Turkish yoke.

The issue has been investigated by historians and scholars ever since. And the verdict appears to be clear. Historian Gunter Lewy:

The three pillars of the Armenian claim to classify World War I deaths as genocide fail to substantiate the charge that the Young Turk regime intentionally organized massacres. Other alleged evidence for a premeditated plan for annihilation fares no better.[48]

Historian Edward J. Erickson:

Many historians find military chronicles dry and difficult to comprehend. Nevertheless, when it comes to controversy over the fate of Armenians in 1915, they are crucial. Many contemporary historians accuse the Special Organization and Major Stange of complicity in genocide. The records, though, do not lend such accusations credence.[49]

Historian Norman Stone:

The Armenian lobby contends that these independent and highly esteemed historians are simply "Ottomanists"—a ridiculously arrogant dismissal. Unfortunately, the issue has never reached a properly constituted court. If the Armenians were convinced of their own case, they would have taken it to one. Instead, they lobby bewildered or bored parliamentary assemblies to "recognize the genocide." Congress should not take a position, one way or the other, on this affair. Let historians decide. The Turkish government has been saying this for years.[50]

But Norman Stone notwithstanding, it is as sure a thing as the sun rising again that, come April 2010, the Congress of the United States will go through its regular spasmodic motions. Once again, members of Congress—Adam B. Schiff, George Radanovich, Frank Pallone, Jr., and Mark Steven Kirk—will write to the president on the upcoming ninety-fifth anniversary of the Armenian Remembrance Day and try to have him say the fateful word. They will be joined by the House speaker Nancy Pelosi and many others, all trying to make political hay on the back of the historical misery of the Armenians.

Of course, the new vice president must not be ignored either. Beginning in 1990, Joe Biden has actively supported all the pro-Armenian resolutions submitted in the Senate. In 1992, he supported the Freedom Support Act that aimed to restrict U.S. assistance to Azerbaijan. He even supported the invasion of Nagorno-Karabakh by Armenia. Biden, in the past, openly admitted that the ultimate goal must be the recognition by Turkey as genocide of the events of

1915 rather than their recognition as genocide by the United States. So what will it be?

In 2009, Barack Obama artfully ducked the issue by saying "it" without saying it. In a statement he issued on Armenian Remembrance Day, he used the Armenian word ("Meds Yeghern") and thus managed to satisfy the irrational desire of the Turkish diplomacy:

> Ninety-four years ago, one of the great atrocities of the 20th century began. Each year, we pause to remember the 1.5 million Armenians who were subsequently massacred or marched to their death in the final days of the Ottoman Empire. The *Meds Yeghern* must live on in our memories, just as it lives on in the hearts of the Armenian people.

Now for 2010, the bar has been raised a notch higher. In fact, during a December 7, 2009, visit to the White House, it has been reported that Erdoğan has been put on notice that come April 2010, the U.S. president will not be able to convince the U.S. House of Representatives to table the "genocide" resolution unless the protocols detailing a comprehensive framework for the normalization of Turkish-Armenian relations and the reopening of the common border, which were agreed upon in Zurich, Switzerland, are adopted by the Turkish parliament.

Ironically, Erdoğan has, on numerous occasions—including during an interview with Charlie Rose[51]—admitted that he does not have the votes to get the protocols adopted by the Turkish parliament unless significant progress in the negotiations between Armenia and Azerbaijan regarding Nagorno-Karabakh and the occupied Azeri territories is reported.

Even though the appearance of an impasse is the logical conclusion, when it comes to predicting the future moves of the present Turkish leadership, all bets are off. Turkish Islamists have, in the past, regularly caved in to outside pressures from the European Union and the United States, and quite effortlessly. So a future AKP policy regarding Azerbaijan is not an easy one to predict. Indeed, here is what Abdullah Gül, the current president of the republic, had to say in 1993, when he was the foreign affairs spokesman for the Refah, the Islamist party du jour on the occasion of a visit by the then Armenian president to Ankara to attend the funeral of the late president Özal:

> With its present policy this government has mortgaged our future. As a result, the Armenian President has dared attend the funeral of the President. He knows that when Turkish national interests are at stake, you will not act like a hawk . . . [S]omeone

who claims Kars to be Armenian territory will come to visit Turkey
and you will shake hands with him.

How much an influence some leading players will have on this and other
issues dividing Turkey and the United States remains to be seen. One influential
player is Vice President Joe Biden. He has had very close relations with ethnic
lobbies—Greek, Armenian, Israeli, and Kurdish—present in the United States.
As a senator, he has mostly voted in line with those ethnic lobbies. Over the
years, the Greek-American senator Paul Sarbanes and Joe Biden have managed
to halt or delay arm sales to Turkey. His position on the issue of the Greek
Orthodox Theological Seminary in Khalki (Heybeliada) and the division of
Cyprus has been pro-Greek. On the issue of Armenian-Turkish relations, Joe
Biden has consistently supported the Armenian genocide claims.

Another player who will have a say on these issues is the secretary of state
Hillary Clinton. During the presidential campaign of 2008, she made no bones
about where she stood on the issue:

> Alone among the Presidential candidates, I have been a
> longstanding supporter of the Armenian Genocide Resolution. I
> have been a co-sponsor of the Resolution since 2002, and I support
> adoption of this legislation by both Houses of Congress. I believe
> the horrible events perpetrated by the Ottoman Empire against
> Armenians constitute a clear case of genocide.[52]

Aram Hamparian, executive director of the Armenian National Committee
of America (ANCA), applauded Hillary Clinton's statement:

> We are certainly pleased to see that, for the first time in recent
> memory, an individual with a strong record in support of Armenian
> Genocide recognition will serve as America's Secretary of State.

Bryan Ardouny, executive director of the Armenian Assembly of America
(AAA), declared,

> Never before have we had such an alignment whereby the
> incoming President, Vice President and Secretary of State have
> a clear and demonstrated record of support for affirmation of the
> Armenian genocide, as well as genocide prevention.

Finally, let us not ignore another political opportunist who has regularly courted Armenian votes and money. House Speaker Nancy Pelosi (D-CA) has been a regular champion of the resolution recognizing the Armenian genocide. She has vowed to bring the measure to a vote since she became speaker. During an official visit to Washington, D.C., by the then Turkish foreign minister Abdullah Gül, Speaker Pelosi rejected Gül's request for a meeting. Unfortunately for her, in the past, she had not been very effective in meddling in foreign policy. However, April 2010 could well be the year she gets what she wants.

Faced with a ferocious anti-Turkish assault by powerful lobbies both here as well as across the Atlantic, only a fiercely independent and resolute Turkish government will be able to defend and protect vital Turkish national interests. Unfortunately, the present Turkish administration is a weak and supplicant regime deserving of the term "client state."

What is essential is to understand that the adoption of such a resolution will only be the opening salvo of a much more determined lobbying effort to pressure the U.S. Congress and other nations to force Turkey to pay reparations and return land to Armenia for genocide not proven in a court of law. Indeed, these demands have already begun to be formulated soon after the announcement of a tentative deal normalizing relations between Armenia and Turkey. During an interview with the Italian television Channel 3 (RAI3) Şahnur Aznavuryan (a.k.a. Charles Aznavour), the eighty-five-year-old French singer who is currently holding the title of Armenian Ambassador to Bern, Switzerland, declared,

> In 1924, the year I was born, Armenians were promised the return of their land. It has not yet been fulfilled. I cannot wait for another 85 years.[53]

The singer obviously was referring to the infamous Treaty of Sevres, which, following WWI, proposed to carve out of the remains of the Ottoman Empire territories to be annexed to France, Great Britain, Kurdistan, Armenia, Greece, and Italy. Others have been equally expansive in their quest for the "lost lands of Armenia." Edgar Hilsenrath in his novel *Das märchen vom letzten gedanken* (The story of the last thought)[54] for which he was awarded the State Award for Literature by the president of the Republic of Armenia, claims that

> 90% of the names of historical Armenia have been changed, only major cities—Van, Bitlis, Erzurum—etc. have been spared . . . Urfa, Diyarbakır, Konya, and Sıvas . . . they all belong to the Armenians.

Cyprus and Greek-Turkish Relations

There are several contentious issues between Greece and Turkey, but none more acute than the problem of divided Cyprus. It has been poisoning EU-Turkey relations ever since 2004 when Turkey was granted the status of candidate member by the Council of the European Union. Prime Minister R. T. Erdoğan, under intense pressure by the Europeans and clearly desirous of securing his flank against the secularist forces in Turkey, signed, in the dead of night, a protocol that, at the time, he and his advisors failed to grasp the significance of. Now the chickens are coming to roost.

On February 18, 2008, the Council of the European Union has decided that under short-term priorities, Turkey must

- actively support efforts to implement the agreed 8th July process leading to a comprehensive and viable settlement of the Cyprus problem within the UN framework and in line with the principles on which the EU is founded, including concrete steps to contribute to a favorable climate for such a comprehensive settlement;
- implement fully the protocol adapting the Ankara Agreement to the accession of the new EU member states, *including* removal of all existing restrictions on *Cyprus-flagged vessels and vessels serving the Cyprus trade*; and
- take concrete steps for the normalization of bilateral relations between Turkey and all EU member states, *including the Republic of Cyprus*, as soon as possible.

As stated above, the EU expects Turkey to honor a pledge made by Erdoğan in Brussels some six years ago. But this the prime minister cannot deliver. Unfortunately, the calendar of events are marching inexorably toward a denouement that could either solve the Cyprus conflict by reuniting the two parts of the Island under a single flag (equivalent, for most Turks, to a sellout) or by making permanent the division (equivalent to a final curtain to Turkey's aspirations to join the EU).

Now, the union of the north and the south of the island is a solution that will depend, to a large degree, on one man: Mehmet Ali Talat, the current president of the Turkish Republic of Northern Cyprus. His term of office will soon expire. Given the balance of power among the various Turkish factions, he has almost no chance of being reelected. Therefore, he faces a very brief period during which time he desperately would like to secure an agreement with his Greek counterpart that would enable Greek voters to participate in the election in the north and vice versa. The modality of such elections, of course, will be very controversial, leading some to accuse Talat of a sellout to the Greeks.

The Turkish prime minister's role in the ongoing negotiations is a risky one. Any appearance of support for Talat's position will, inevitably, be construed as a sellout on his part too.

Another hot and contentious topic is the fate of the Khalki (Heybeliada) Theological Seminary, which the patriarch Bartholomew I would like to see reopen. The issue has added another dimension to the old and festering debate about the recognition by the Turkish government of the "ecumenical" title associated with the patriarch's name.

The ecumenical patriarchate in Istanbul (historically Constantinople) dates from the Greek Orthodox Byzantine Empire, which collapsed in 1453, when the city fell to the Ottoman Turks. Bartholomew I says he represents the world's 300 million Orthodox Christians as a "first among equals." However, the Turkish government—pointing to a clause in the Lausanne Treaty, which was signed between Greece and Turkey following the Greek-Turkish war of 1919-1922—withholds recognition of the patriarch's ecumenical title, treating him only as the spiritual leader of the Orthodox Greeks still living in Turkey.

The reopening of the seminary and the future of the patriarchate are interrelated. Previous prime ministers have, on several occasions, offered to open the seminary as part of a faculty of theology, within any one of the local universities. In order to prevent a mushrooming of madrassa-style uncontrolled religious education, the Turkish constitution has specifically addressed the issue and thus requires such training to be the purview of an institution of higher learning. Nevertheless, one cannot help but sympathize with the patriarch's predicament. Here is the dilemma: The youngest Greek Orthodox presently domiciled in Istanbul is sixty years old, and the pool from which the future priests will be drawn is shrinking rather dramatically. It would not be too far-fetched to say that within a decade or two, the Greek minority will dwindle to less than a thousand at the most. The specter of a church with no parishioners may be what prompted ecumenical patriarch Bartholomew I to say, on the CBS *60 Minutes* program, that in Turkey he feels "crucified" and a "second-class citizen." Needless to say, the comments were enough to create a firestorm of mutual recrimination. Foreign Minister Ahmet Davutoğlu, during a press conference, said, "We cannot accept comparisons that we do not deserve." Greece hit back the next day. Greece's foreign ministry responded by immediately playing the best card they held:

> Among Turkey's obligations for joining the European Union,
> the respect for the freedom of religion and the rights of minorities
> takes first place.

The issue of the rights of minorities is another reference point to which one has to seek an answer by looking, once again, into the Treaty of Lausanne, which ended the conflict between Greece and Turkey. In it, the treaty stipulates that whatever rights Turkey grants to its non-Muslim minorities are being equally granted by Greece to its Muslim minorities (Article 43: Minority Rights). So it is time some fair and objective observers begin to look at the plight of the Muslim minorities living in Western Thrace.

As can be assessed from the topics presented above, the EU has, until now, been the dominant and mostly domineering element of Turkish foreign policy. However, most recently, a breath of fresh air appears to be seeping through the crack of the Islamist foreign policy, which up until now, to put it simply and bluntly, had been nothing but the policy of a supplicant at the gate of Europe.

The new Turkish foreign minister, Ahmet Davutoglu, has introduced a nuanced yet significant twist in his approach to the EU as well as to the Middle East and Eurasia.

In his magisterial work *Stratejik derinlik* (Strategic depth), he calls for an "identity renewal," which he believes will overcome the centuries-old Turkish obsession over Europe versus Asia syndrome (translated from Turkish by SS):

> Turkey, a country at the intersection of Eurasia's East-West and North-South axes must overcome the influence of a meaningless distinction over its being European or Asiatic and proceed to develop a long-term strategy. The geo-cultural infrastructure for such a strategy would call for Turkey to enter a period of thorough identity renewal which would represent a major foundation of such an infrastructure.

But the Turkish foreign minister's most revealing observations and conclusions pertain to his warning regarding the future of Turkey within EU if and when certain conditions, as he outlines, are not met:

> An approach reducing and limiting Turkey's economy and its international economic relations into a EU frame of reference is like throwing an arrow, without the use of a bow, in an unknown direction. Thus, not only is there an absence of a rational relationship between the arrow and the target but, also the motivation of the society, so

---

essential for developing the launching power of the bow, would not be secured.

A Turkey unable to plant both feet solidly on the Asiatic soil will have difficulty to set his eyes and its horizon focused on Europe. Just as Ottoman thrust into Europe suffered during each period of crisis, similarly, a Turkey who has failed to mobilize its economic and political potential in Asia, would have no other chance nor choice other than be a market or touristic venue within the EU.[55]

This is as compelling and profound and argument as one can make in defense of an independent foreign policy.

Shifting Axes: Arab Middle East vs. NATO-EU-USA

During the Davos Forum of 2009, Prime Minister Erdoğan displayed an uncontrolled temper tantrum against the Israeli president Shimon Peres. It might have been unrehearsed but certainly had profound policy implications abroad. A few months later, Prof. Mehmet Davutoğlu, a newcomer, took over the helm of the Turkish foreign policy establishment. He might have concluded that the Davos debacle was just the right impetus he needed to shift the axis of Turkish foreign policy from its decades-old NATO-EU-USA axis to a new and more flexible one centered around his concept of "strategic depth."

It is conceivable that Dr. Davutoğlu and his team have reached the conclusion, and a right one, that Turkish dream of accession into EU was just that, a pipe dream, and that Turkey better reorient its foreign policy axis, seeking other partners and strategic alliances. Since then, the Syrian-Turkish rapprochement has culminated in the removal of visa requirements for travel and the introduction of the term "strategic" to define the new relationship. In a more recent visit to Russia, the term "strategic" has been used by prime ministers Erdoğan and Putin to describe their mutual relationship.

Furthermore, Turkey's economic landscape may have contributed to a more nuanced approached in its foreign policy toward the Arab Middle East. Especially, the lure of petrodollars sloshing around in search of acquisitions may have been the inspiration for the Turkish government's proposed sale, in the coming years, of bridges, highways, and many other infrastructure projects, all in the hope of covering a massive balance of payment deficit, which is growing by leaps and bounds.

A foreign policy reversal of this magnitude, coupled with an Israeli response that proved to be rude and crude (by inviting the Turkish ambassador to the foreign office and deliberately insulting him before a slew of news cameras), has its rewards too. Indeed the anti-Israeli sentiments it generated had improved significantly the prime minister's poll number.

There is one problem, though. It stems from the fact that if interpreted in a very simplistic way, as being turning away from the West, then the consequences of such a policy shift could prove disastrous. I suspect that the prime minister is misreading the true significance of the policy and thus falls prey to a demagogic display of independence, which translates into temper tantrums such as those he continues to make regarding Gazza and his friendship toward Ahmadinejad. For the prime minister, the shift is more ideologic than strategic whereas for the foreign minister, it is simply strategic.

4

Culture of Corruption

"Turkey is defecating. Turkey will continue cleansing its intestines."[56] So says Mehmet Ali Şahin, Turkey's minister of justice and senior member of the ruling Islamist AKP, referring to an ongoing "cleansing" scam called Ergenekon, a long, interminable saga of arrests, searches, seizures, and gross constitutional violations of human rights of anti-Islamists and left wing intellectuals, some of whom are behind bars for almost two years while others are still waiting to be charged after over eighteen months of incarceration. Others may wish to disagree with the minister:

> Beyond the looking glass in the Republic of Turkey, almost a hundred suspects have been swept up in raids, predawn and otherwise, to be held without benefit of provisions of habeas corpus. Some were held without charges upwards of 18 months. Some died in prison, uncharged. A few were released. Ripe with the odor of a fishing expedition—documents confiscated, computers impounded and subject to being loaded with false evidence—the so-called investigation marches on, a legally blind beast of terror. So-called evidence is leaked to the public by the religious, pro-government press. Human rights? The rule of law? Not in Wonderland Turkey. Not through Turkey's looking glass.[57]

The sad reality is that Turkey today is in the grip of a widespread network of corruption that is eating the flesh and soul of the nation. Piece by piece, they are selling off the homestead we inherited. A large-scale epidemic of bribery of government officials, embezzlement by high-powered bureaucrats, blackmail, extortion, violence, drug racketeering, and white-color crime provides the backdrop for a canvas of poverty and massive unemployment. What makes this picture scary is the fact that the Islamist regime and its leaders have, since the days when the prime minister was the mayor of Istanbul, engaged in corrupt and sleazy activities. The premier industrialist of Turkey, Rahmi Koç—during an interview on *CNN Türk*, broadcast on August 3, 2001—claimed that

Tayyip Erdoğan was a billionaire! Erdoğan never refuted the statement by the businessman and has often pointed to the gifts presented at his son's circumcision as the main source of his fortune. Poor as he was when he first landed in Istanbul as a young aspiring professional soccer player, he was helped by his friends before he could buy his first soccer shoes. Today he remains shielded behind parliamentary immunity from the numerous charges leveled against him during his tenure as mayor of Istanbul. Since his ascendancy to the prime minister's office, the accusations of nepotism, favoritism toward certain businessmen via no-bid contracts, and corrupt practices have never been properly answered as he continues to enjoy immunity from prosecution.

In order to appreciate the premeditated nature of these events, we need to look at some early actions taken by the Islamist regime. Following their electoral victory in the November 2002 elections, the AKP majority ram through a bill that should have given us a hint of the future. On January 2003, the official gazette published the cornerstone of the upcoming highway robbery. Article 30/7 of the Turkish Law regarding taxing procedures and Article 82/2 of the Turkish Income Tax Code were annulled via the adoptions of Articles 7 and 9 of Parliament Bill No. 4783. The bill made it impossible to question the source of the wealth of the son or daughter or wife of an elected official. In short, the days of "where, when, and how?" became history.

Following the adoption of the bill, Turkey saw an influx of large but dirty money of questionable origin. Money laundering had become a big, very big business. We were witnessing the coming of age of some very young and rather very successful sons and daughters of the powerful and of the politically well connected. Ahmet Burak Erdoğan, the thirty-year-old son of Prime Minister Erdoğan had become the proud owner of a million-dollar villa and, a year later, of a container ship capable of transporting two hundred containers. The thirty-year-old son of a cabinet minister owned a €30 million factory, several real estate properties, and had a controlling interest in several corporations. His overall worth was estimated to be about $50-100 million.[58] [59]

In 2004, AKP-sponsored legislation aimed at reducing the value-added tax (VAT) on the sale of precious stones such as diamond, emerald, pearl, and ruby from 18 percent to 0 percent. What, at the time, seemed rather bizarre, now, with the benefit of knowing that a close friend of the prime minister was a trader of precious stone, became more understandable.[60] It became even more so when it was divulged that it was the same friend, Cihan Kamer, who was involved in the famous transaction reported by the prime minister as part of the source of his fortune: the sale, to Mr. Kamer, of the gold and other precious gems presented to the family on the occasion of their daughter's wedding.

In a land where bread, cheese, olive, milk, egg, water, and, yes, even the shroud for a deceased is subject to a value-added tax, it is incomprehensible and callous to eliminate it for such luxury items. However, when a culture of corruption envelops a country, especially a country where inequalities of wealth and disparities of sacrifice are enormous, such policies will reflect only the true face of a regime determined to enrich its cronies at the expense of the less-fortunate members of the nation.

Consider the appalling conditions prevailing throughout the southeast of Turkey. In Diyarbakır alone, there are over twenty thousand families living with an annual income of $350, which is less than $1 a day. These families are in desperate need for food. According to a World Bank report highlighting income inequality, the percentage of those living below the internationally recognized poverty limit of less than $2 a day has reached 24.7 percent of the Turkish population. This number is 2 percent in Poland, 7.5 percent in Russia, 14.3 percent in Argentina, and 22.4 percent in Brazil. And yet, the wealth of politicians contrast sharply with the immediate poverty of the people they profess to represent. The country is ranked near bottom of the UN Development Programme's Human Development Index.

The social dislocations are compounded by the increase in unemployment. In October 2009, nonfarm unemployment in Turkey has swelled to 16.3 percent; and even more worrisome, the number of unemployed youth is now 23.2 percent of the Turkish workforce. And yet, the circus continues.

A state refinery (Tüpraş) valued at about $50 billion was sold, a few years ago, for $1.3 billion. It was alleged that $400 million in bribe money was paid to secure the contract. A case that, according to legal experts, was dripping of illegalities and graft! The Erdoğan government had indeed disqualified several solid competitors for various dubious reasons but had insisted that a Turkish contractor, a close friend of the prime minister, be included as partner in the team, which eventually was awarded the contract. Later on, when it was announced that the winning group was trying to secure credit for 70 percent of the total bid, no one was surprised. For many observers of the Turkish scene, this sale will probably be one of the central corruption charges that will be leveled against Erdoğan if and when he no longer is protected by parliamentary immunity.

There is, however, a more recent case. It has been in the news for over a year although the events leading to it goes far back. It has an international flavor for the embezzlement charges have been brought not in Turkey but in Germany.

On April 2007, German Prosecutor Kerstin Lötz indicted three officials of Deniz Feneri e.V., a Turkish charity in Germany, for embezzlement of millions of euros of donated funds and funneling them to Islamist companies operating in Turkey. On September17, 2008, Frankfurt State High Court president Johann Mueller handed down a prison sentence of five years and ten months for one of the accused and two years and nine months for another. The third suspect was given a suspended sentence. What made the case so relevant to the corruption cases tossed around in Turkey was what the judge said during sentencing. In the opinion of the German judge, the masterminds of the fraud were in Turkey. Mueller said that the accused former director of the charity was merely a pawn directed from Turkey. He added that the head of the Turkish media watchdog, RTÜK, Zahid Akman, was implicated in the affair and that Zekeriya Karaman, one of the founders of Deniz Feneri Turkey (a sister charity operating in Turkey) and the executive board chairman of the Islamist Kanal 7 TV, has had a leading role in the fraud. According to press reports, donations were allegedly used to fund companies with ties to Prime Minister Erdoğan. Critics accuse the government and prime minister of protecting the accomplices in the affair and using the embezzled money to support the AKP and its political agenda. Leading Deniz Feneri representatives are AKP members, and the opposition maintains that the money was used to finance media close to the AKP, and part of it may have ended up in the coffer of the party itself.

Following the disposition of the case against Deniz Feneri e.V. the prosecutor's office in Frankfurt has filed a case against the man the judge had accused to be one of the masterminds of the previous case, Zahid Akman, on the charge of aggravated fraud. The dossier of the Deniz Feneri e.V. is now in the hands of the Turkish Ministry of Justice. However, after nearly a year, four months of which were spent translating the files at snail's pace, no action has so far been observed; and none is expected!

Although, in the past seven years, Turkey has made significant economic progress, much of this has since unraveled amid egregious graft, massive corruption, and favoritism, a poisonous mix that has brought the country to the brink of chaos. A close-knit religious elite—mainly the followers of the Naqshibendi order and those of Fethullah Gülen—joined forces with a corrupt oligarchy to create what Larry Diamond calls a predatory state using the power of patronage, coercion, and demagogic electoral appeals to religious pride and prejudice. According to Larry Diamond, "[t]he most egregious predatory states produce predatory societies. People do not get rich through productive activities and honest risk taking; they get rich by manipulating power and privilege, by stealing from the state, extracting from the weak, and shirking the law. Political actors in predatory societies use any means necessary and break any rules possible in their quest for power and wealth."[61]

It is safe to say that the above is an accurate description of the present state of affairs in Turkey. What is more telling is his observation that Western leaders tend to speak out only when democratic norms are violated by unfriendly governments and soft-pedal abuses when allies are involved.

The AKP administration has earned a reputation for being the most scandal tainted in the history of Turkey. Political and business figures whose ethics were, at best, highly dubious have brought this regime to one of the lowest points of the republic. A storybook of scandals, a veritable tome of venality, a catalog of corruption, egregious violations of the public trust, and wide-scale thievery has been going on unchecked for the past eight years.

Ismet Berkan writing for the daily *Radikal* has detailed three such events in three consecutive articles where he carefully described the consuming greed and corruption of certain officials in some "unnamed country." Freedom of the press being a rather-forgotten concept lately, it is understandable that he couched his story in rather nonspecific terms.[62]

The first story describes the sale of a highly valued public company (a state refinery?) by the government as part of its privatization program. The initial sale attracts very many bidders, but the authorities decide to cancel it on the ground that it is not competitive enough. A second sale invitation attracts, once again, a large number of interested parties, both national and international. But there is a hitch. The government agency in charge of the bidding process finds that foreign ownership of the said company, given the sector in which it operates, will not be possible under the present law. And the government displays no interest whatsoever in amending the old law. Foreign companies now realize that they are not welcome to bid, and they withdraw. This leaves the scene to a few local entrepreneurs. One of these companies (we'll call them A) appears to be the most qualified when compared to the rest. But there is another interested party (we'll call them B). Company B is well known to be very close to the regime, and they go around town bragging that the bid will be theirs.

In the meantime, the administrator of the public authority directing the bidding process declares to a television station that no bid less than a specific amount will be considered. The amount uttered by the administrator is well beyond the resources of company B. A few weeks later, someone representing B approaches A and proposes a partnership. Bidder A consents to the partnership and inquires about their respective shares of the new company. Bidder B tells A that they will own a 30 percent share of the new partnership with a payment of only 15 percent. When A then asks when they will pay the remainder 15 percent of the deal, the response is straightforward. Party B has no intention of paying the remaining 15 percent. They remind their new potential partner that instead of the 15 percent payment, they will bring to the deal their close association with the government.

Bidder A is no fool. They decide not to partake in such a charade. The sole actor left on the scene is the weakest of them all. Indeed, most observers have judged B to be unqualified to even participate in the auction. Next, the winner party B begins to develop special ties with the government by employing relatives of several cabinet members in upper-echelon positions within the company. The final contract is signed and sealed after the government actively directs some public banks to provide the necessary letters of credits.

Let us fast-forward to a meeting the prime minister of the country is having with some newspaper reporters. When the topic of conversation centers about the said company and the businessman friend, the prime minister becomes very agitated. His fury is directed against the head of the public authority that directed the sale. He accuses him of discouraging potential bidders by declaring a too-high opening bid. Ismet Berkan concludes that it appeared as if the prime minister wished that the public company had been sold to a private entity for a lot lesser price.

Another newspaperman, when told about the above conversation, becomes intrigued. He begins digging. What he uncovers during his investigations is scary. The prime minister has been personally involved in the negotiations dealing with money and company shares!

Ismet Berkan's next story[63] of corruption in high places is, once again, the tale of a sale, by a government agency, of a public company (Telekom?) valued at several billions of dollars. It was an event that was supposed to attract world-class companies operating in the same field. The winning bid was expected to fetch several billions of dollars. Among the parties interested in the sale, one noted the presence of a company owned by the former prime minister of a neighboring country (Lebanon?).

The former prime minister, well aware of how things are handled in the region, sets out to find a powerful (i.e., influential) partner. Having drawn a list of such potential partners, he meets one-on-one with each and every one of them. But strangely enough, none of those interviewed accepts the former prime minister's offer to join in partnership. In one of these conversations, he refers to a foreign journalist (a citizen of a country—Syria?—that occupied the former prime minister's country for very many years) and in a very hush-hush manner (by writing his name on a piece of paper) tells his visitor that said journalist is their conduit to the government.

When the day of bidding arrives, (surprise, surprise) none of the world-class giants submit a bid to this most valuable asset, which is, in fact, a monopoly within the country. So the former prime minister's company secures the winning bid. The new owners proceed to consolidate by planning to dispose of several assets they consider unproductive. Among them, there are several real estate properties offered for sale. An interested party pays a visit to the director general of the new company, inquiring about the sale of some of these assets. The director general tells the businessman that for such matters, he should get in touch with "Abdullah Bey." Who was Abdullah Bey? He has no affiliation with the new company. He runs an import-export business of his own, and in addition, he serves as vice-chairman of the board of directors of a foreign bank specializing in Shariah-compliant banking.

The businessman interested in acquiring some of these real estate properties begins to inquire about Abdullah Bey. He quickly realizes that Abdullah Bey, though he appears to be unaffiliated with the said company, in reality is directly involved in many of their activities; and in some, he is the ultimate decision maker. Further inquiries have divulged that Abdullah Bey may actually be the owner of a 10 percent share of the company even though Abdullah Bey's lifestyle and company records do not indicate such a 10 percent ownership. Could it be that he owns shares in the company's offshore properties? No one knows. In this land, transparency is not de rigueur. Abdullah Bey lives in a modest apartment building where occupants remove their shoes at the entrance door. A truly religious man, he has been rather successful in his import-export business (wheat).

There is another possibility: could he be the reliable cashier of someone who wants, or rather has, to remain anonymous? It is worth remembering that the former prime minister of the neighboring country (he later fell victim of a suicide bombing—Refik Hariri?) must have made thorough investigations before soliciting the services of Abdullah Bey.

Finally, a few observations regarding the business acumen of Abdullah Bey: It is said that although Abdullah Bey has not yet paid any money for his 10 percent share of the deal, he already is exercising his "option." In the meantime, first the shares of the parent company and later those of his company has almost doubled in price. So Abdullah Bey's worth has doubled to a whopping $2 billion even though he hasn't made any payment yet.

Now let us ask ourselves the inevitable questions.

What has made Abdullah Bey a shareholder of such dimension in one of the country's largest corporations? Is it his business acumen? Or is he just a front man holding the money for some others?

Is the story just a simple case of corruption—even though the sums involved may be massive? Or is it something truly sui generis, that of a party (AKP?) feeding from a trough of corruption?

Finally, there is the tale of a bank.[64] It was taken over by the government, and following its reorganization, it was put up for sale as part of the government's privatization program. But no one was willing to bid. As a consequence, the sale was postponed, the opening bid price was lowered, and a new invitation to bid was issued. This time, several bids were submitted. The winner was a corporation headquartered in a neighboring Islamic country. While they were busy preparing the necessary paperwork, a person known to be a close friend of the prime minister went around telling people that the bank was sold "dirt cheap." Had he known that this would be the case, he would have bought it himself! Such talk eventually reached the ear of the government administrator in charge of approving the bid and also of those who were responsible for issuing the appropriate banking license to the new owners.

Panic set in. Questions were raised. Was the person claiming to be interested in the bank speaking with the approval of the prime minister? Was he expressing the views and wishes of the prime minister? No one knew.

But while these rumors are swirling, another one is put into circulation by the friend of the prime minister. He accuses the government agency of bias in favor of the highest bidder and asks that the bid be cancelled.

What is so remarkable is that the head of the government agency in charge of the sale and the friend of the prime minister both belong to the same ideological movement (could it be AKP?), and yet when money and vested interests are involved, they are miles apart. So under intense pressure, the head of the government agency declares that, although he has no authority to annul the bid, the agency responsible for the issuance of the banking license can do so!

When the winning party submits all the pertinent paperwork to the relevant authorities, things begin to slow down. More documents to submit, more paperwork to attend to. Eventually, the curtain falls: the winning bidder's financial resources are found to be inadequate. The contract is annulled. Stay tuned.

In a recent report,[65] the Turkish Chamber of Electrical Engineers (EMO) has described in great detail some of the most recent contract manipulations the administration has put into play in order to force winning contractors to enter into partnerships with some of the Islamic bourgeoisie's new entrepreneurs. According to EMO, prior to the signing of a contract, the new regulation will allow (!) the contractor to form a new partnership with a minority ownership of up to 49 percent. Of course, whether the awarding of the contract was conditioned on the establishment of such a forced marriage was not made clear.

Quo vadis? Ali Bulaç, an ardent Islamist, answered that question a few years ago. "Are the unethical behavior and the irresponsible lifestyles of those in leadership positions and the ideology of this political movement reconcilable? Is this what we call conservative democracy? It is obvious that the house is filled with dirt. You will not be able to remove it by simply shoving it under the furniture and the rugs."[66] He went on further:

> At present, a small clique—a few years ago they were ardent Islamists—are sitting at the head of the spring, holding all power centers, and as they fill their pockets, they belittle and degrade Muslims.[67]

As if there was additional need to confirm the rampant corruption narratives of this army of thieves, on December 26, 2009, we witnessed an AKP deputy from the East (Elazığ), Feyzi İşbaşaran, spilling the beans before all media outlets. Under order from the prime minister, he was about to be taken before an ethics committee with a request that he be expelled from the party. Furious at the manner he was treated—he learned the news while watching television—he made the following statement:

> I have always expressed my opinions freely and openly. I have never remained silent. I am not the one who built, illegally, in the middle of a forestland a villa. I am not the one who arranged for a protocol in exchange for a million-dollar bribe. I am not the one who served as an intermediary during the privatization sale of state assets. I am not the one who walked away with people's money using a flashlight or a Lighthouse. I am not the one who helped the corporation headed by my son acquire a radio or a television station. I am not the one who bought a ship or any other thing for the benefit of my son . . . As a Prime Minister who cannot defend and protect the honor and integrity of a Member of Parliament, how will you be able to defend the country?[68]

In other egregious scandals, armies of voracious dealmakers have moved in for financial killings. Political cronies of the powerful have successfully engineered transactions selling government land at hugely inflated prices and made instant tycoons out of scheming insiders who had been tipped off to the details. Elected municipal party hacks have rezoned agricultural land and proceeded to develop shopping malls.

This government and its cronies have never ceased to siphon off the wealth of the nation. One of the most utterly corrupt, incompetent, nitwitted team in the history of the republic is selling off the homestead we inherited, little by little, piece by piece. With each passing day, the great auction of Turkey's national assets is gaining momentum; and with it, charges of corrupt practices and the misuse of official position for personal gain leveled against the leaders of this Islamist regime are getting more and more voluminous. It is imperative that the law requiring all elected officials to declare the source of their wealth be reintroduced. In the words of Kurt Vonnegut, "Psychopathic personalities, which is to say persons without conscience, without senses of pity or shame, have taken all the money."[69]

5

Democracy Alla Turca

Given a choice between a government without free press and a free press without a government I'd not hesitate a moment to prefer the latter.

—*Thomas Jefferson*

The Footprints of a Fascist

The *Merriam-Webster Dictionary* defines "fascism" as "a political philosophy, movement or regime that exalts 'nation' and often 'race' above individual and that stands for a centralized autocratic government headed by a dictatorial leader, severe economic and social regimentation, and forcible suppression of opposition.

The ruling AKP regime has so far met most, if not all, of the above criteria by

- exalting Islam and seeking the Islamic identity (*umma*),
- establishing a one-man rule and the cult of his personality,
- developing a "heavily armed police unit" to counterbalance the threat of the army,
- controlling the state bureaucracy,
- employing state power to impose a particular order on society,
- muzzling critical media,
- eliminating diverse opinion within the ruling party,
- tolerating the regression of liberal values,
- creating its own pious bourgeoisie by manipulating the "rules of the game."

In fact, you might even conclude that these are not footsteps any longer but rather the footprints of a nascent dictatorship.

"If a country holds competitive, multiparty elections, we call it democratic, [even if] governments produced by [such] elections [are] inefficient, corrupt, shortsighted, irresponsible, dominated by special interests, and incapable of adopting policies demanded by the public."[70] Fareed Zakaria, in his *Foreign Affairs* article, has distinguished between procedures for selecting government (democracy) and the goals of such a government (constitutional liberalism). The latter emphasizes individual liberties and the rule of law. It defends the individual's right to life and property, and freedom of religion and speech. In order to secure these rights, checks on the power of each branch of government must be enforced. Equality under the law and impartiality of the courts must be secured; and secularism, the separation of church and state, must be observed.

Since Turkey regularly holds "competitive, multiparty" elections, which are free and somewhat fair, the question may seem to be reduced to whether it would qualify as a liberal or illiberal democracy. Having described in the preceding chapters the circumstances surrounding the governance of the nation, it seems to be self-evident that at the present the Turkish system is corrupt to the core, and the litmus test is what follows the elections.

In today's Turkey, the rule of law, individual liberties, the freedom of the press and the media, and the independent judiciary are all subject to an intense assault by the regime. The motivation for such an attack is the fear of the future: a regime knee-deep in corruption is beginning to sense that the curtain may someday come down on this orgy. What follows will not look pretty. Just like any cornered wild animal, this regime is using all the forces at its disposal to fend off the approaching tsunami. Foremost among them will be its reliance on the police as a counterweight against the threat from secular groups and, particularly, the threat of a military intervention.

The Islamist regime's attempts to centralize its authority by extraconstitutional means have resulted in a series of clashes with the constitutional court, the superior administrative court (Danıştay), the superior court for fiscal affairs (Sayıştay), and of course the media. Encroaching on and usurping the powers and rights of other elements of the society has become this regime's last mechanism for self-defense.

By muzzling dissent, confiscating property, and threatening opponents through the use of various tax penalties, the regime has indeed become a predatory system. However, there is another mortal danger lurking in the background. Without an established culture of constitutional liberalism, democracy, in divided societies, has actually fomented nationalism and ethnic conflict. As Fareed Zakaria has pointed out,

[e]lections require that politicians compete for people's votes. In societies without strong traditions of multiethnic groups or assimilation, it is easiest to organize support along racial, ethnic, or religious lines.[71]

Now that scenario is a very accurate description of the present state of affairs in Turkey. The majority AKP looks for support along religious lines. The pro-Kurdish DTP played the ethnic card until the constitutional court finally decided to shut it down. And, of course, the Nationalist Movement Party (MHP) has always appealed to the extreme nationalist voters. By manipulating the minimum requirement for parliamentary representation (10 percent of the nationwide vote is the threshold), the majority has always managed to keep certain ethnic groups from securing a voice in the political arena. The unintended consequence of this corrupt process finally came to bite those who had engineered it. In the 2002 general election, the religious right garnered 34 percent of the vote but secured 66 percent of the parliamentary seats. Fairness in representation at the national level must be achieved by lowering the threshold to a reasonable 5 or 6 percent of the nationwide vote. Only then can Turkish parliament begin to claim to represent the will of the people.

Religious reactionary movements have, since the birth of the republic, threatened the survival of most of the reforms adopted by Kemal Atatürk and his colleagues. Particularly threatened is the secular nature of the young republic. That threat has not diminished; on the contrary, it has never been greater. A cardinal pillar of constitutional liberalism, secularism today is, in Turkey, the only serious roadblock against the victory of political Islam. The slow but systematic erosion of the wall separating religious and political domains, if unchecked, will inevitably lead to the undoing of all that was achieved as part of the Kemalist revolution.

Western powers and especially the United States have recently adopted a rather tolerant view of a moderately Islamic Turkish Republic as opposed to what the Turkish constitution requires, namely a secular one. They desire to present the face of a modern, democratic, and yet moderate Islamic state to the nations of the Middle East as a model of an Islamic society genuinely adapted to the modern era. The danger is that any such interpretation would imply that under such definition, the social, economic, political, and legal frameworks under which the Turkish State operates would be to a certain measure governed by Qur'anic principles. In my definition, that would be a reactionary retreat for the Kemalist revolution. However, it is no secret that, that is precisely what the present Islamist regime has adopted as an undeclared agenda. Those advocating for Turkey to be a moderate Islamic model must be reminded that the transformation from moderate to radical is an inevitable trend, and at the end of that road, the first victim has always been democracy itself.

The same internal and external elements plotting to erode the secular character of the Turkish Republic have also been actively involved in undermining the nation's control of its own natural resources and its means of production by privatizing most of these resources. Privatization, as discussed before, has been, for the leaders of the majority party, a rather lucrative opportunity. They have not only enriched themselves but at the same time also secured powerful friends and patrons. The true nature of the devastation caused by the wholesale selling of the major infrastructure projects of the republic has been described, lately, by none other than Abdüllatif Şener. As vice-premier, he was the man in charge of the privatization program, but he refused to go along with the prime minister's directives; and as a result, the privatization board ceased to report to him. Addressing workers on strike at the Turkish State Tobacco Corporation, he stated that the government's privatization policies and its attempts to sell to private corporations most of the state-owned industries have been wrongheaded from top to bottom. He reminded his audience that during the period when he was in charge of the privatization program, he had not endorsed any one of the major privatization efforts. He blasted the program as an economic model imposed by the international capital:

> The attitude of the Prime Minister reflects an ideology. It is the ideology of international capital. The Prime Minister is of the opinion that borders have lost any meaning, and that anyone can go anywhere they wish and do business. Such an understanding exists nowhere. It is only this Prime Minister and this government that is selling anything and everything to foreigners. Banks, Telekom, the State Telephone Monopoly, State Tobacco Monopoly, and various strategic industries have passed into the hands of international corporations by being privatized. Next, two of the major state-owned Banks, Ziraat Bankası and Halk Bankası, are on the chopping block along with autoroutes, bridges, The State Lottery and numerous Hydroelectric Power plants. The Prime Minister, by delivering major sectors of the economy into the hands of international capital has ruined the Turkish economy.[72]

former vice-premier reminded his listeners that the unemployment rate in Turkey was hovering around 30 percent and that the economy the prime minister talked about was his own. His final words: "They are finishing off this country!"

Already in the 1970s, the chronic deficit in the balance of payments of what Ernst Mandel called the semicolonies was compensated by so-called development aid, but this aid was merely revealing its character as state assistance to the monopolies exporting machines from the "imperialist" countries. According to Mandel,[73]

> for such grants lead in turn to a growing burden of debt, so that an increasing portion of the total returns on exports of the semi-colonies must be converted into interest re-exported to the metropolitan states.

> At the end of 1972, debt service absorbed . . . 18.8% of the export revenues of Turkey. At the same time the penetration of imperialist capital into the manufacturing industry of the semi-colonies and its growing fusion with the indigenous capital of the so-called "national bourgeoisie" mean that an increasing proportion of capital ownership in these countries falls into the hands of the imperialist concerns (even if this is often camouflaged by local straw men of various form of joint ventures, often combined with state, national or international institutions.)

> This process is accompanied by a disguised capital outflow in such forms as high payment for international experts and technicians.

The above narrative is a remarkably accurate and prescient description of the current state of the Turkish economy. The inescapable and sad conclusion to draw is that after more than thirty-eight years since Mandel's assessment, Turkey will still fit the description he offered for a semicolony state. Indeed, today's Turkish economy is that of a nonproducing society. Unemployment is far greater than what it was during the 1994 and 2001 crises. The big winners are the foreign investors manipulating the local stock exchange, and the big loser is the industrial base of the country. Turkey has the dubious honor of holding the record for the most expensive gasoline, diesel fuel, and liquid propane gas. The cotton and tobacco growers and those whose main business has been the raising of livestock have all been devastated.

One would assume that such topics would be the subject of vigorous debates in the Turkish Grand National Assembly. Unfortunately, the fact of the matter is, with its overwhelming majority and its domineering command over that majority, the prime minister and its cabinet have effectively reduced the parliament to a silent majority.

That brings us to another serious flaw in the Turkish democratic process. The selection of the candidates for parliament is left to each party's leadership. To expect independent and candid opinion from such a docile and captive group is unrealistic. Democracy will not, indeed cannot, flourish at the national if it is not adopted and enforced at the local level. The whole process is emblematic of the mistrust the party leaders have of the cadres working at the precinct and provincial levels.

Finally, we must address the Achilles' heel of the Turkish democracy: the miserable level of primary and secondary education in certain parts of the country. Inequality in the delivery of basic education to young generations eventually translates into illiterate or semi-illiterate masses incapable of reading or writing adequately and, as a result, of understanding the significance of what they read. The present Islamist regime has, ever since they assumed power, aimed at elevating the stature of the Imam-Hatip schools and remove all the obstacles preventing them from successfully participating in university entrance exams. The Imam-Hatip schools were initially conceived as training ground for future Imams to be appointed to various mosques around the country. The need for such employment is limited. However, the state has not only opened thousands of such schools, but it has also allowed the enrollment of girls. Since women are not supposed to serve as Imam, the schools are no longer purely a "technical" institution preparing young men for a profession. The ruse worked effectively. Modern-day madrassas have taken their place among the Turkish educational institutions governed by a ministry of education who was, for the most part of seven years, directed by a member of the Naqshibendi brotherhood.

Established in 1923, the Turkish Republic proceeded immediately to reform the education system by closing, in 1924, all madrassas and religious orders and brotherhoods (*zaviye, tekke, tariqat*). The fundamental law governing education in the land (dated March 3, 1924) called for a unitary education system, thus abolishing the religious education as an option. It is the cornerstone of Turkish secular education and the target of Islamist enmity. It can be said that the day Islamists succeed in emasculating the nation's unitary education will be the day when constitutional liberalism will cease to exist in Turkey. Current attempts by the administration to accommodate the graduates of Imam-Hatip schools by recognizing the equivalence of their curricula to those of the Turkish state high schools (Lise) are just one of many such moves destined to tear down the secular wall separating the mosque and the state. The truth is that what was supposed to have been abolished in 1924, i.e., the religious orders (*tariqat*), have survived all those years and now are surfacing in a major way. The Naqshibendi religious order, along with the brotherhood lead by Fethullah Gülen, is part and parcel of today's ruling oligarchy. Having successfully infiltrated the upper echelons of the state security apparatus, today they are a force to recon with. The likelihood of them branching out and forming (à la Egyptian Muslim brotherhood) some form of paramilitary movement is not totally out of the realm of possibility. They are backed by powerful Islamic holding companies with vast financial resources at their disposal. The hierarchy under which the religious orders do operate and the lack of tolerance they display are incompatible with the modern concepts of democracy and constitutional liberalism. They may be best described as some form of religious mafia.

How to distinguish a democracy that is true from a sham one is a subject worth debating. Ronald Inglehardt and Christian Welzel write,

> Initially, there was a tendency to view any regime that held free and fair elections as a democracy. But many of the new democracies suffered from massive corruption and failed to apply the rule of law, which is what makes democracy effective. A growing number of observers today thus emphasize the inadequacy of "electoral democracy," "hybrid democracy," "authoritarian democracy," and other forms of sham democracy in which mass preferences are something that political elites can largely ignore and in which they do not decisively influence government decisions. It is important, accordingly, to distinguish between effective and ineffective democracies.[74]

It is fair to say that democracy and constitutional liberalism are not doing well in today's Turkey. As the late Ahmet Taner Kışlalı so aptly described,[75]

> If democrat are those who are engaged in the politics and selling of religion, then I am not a democrat!

> . . . If democracy is the name of the system which protects the liars, the thieves and all those on the payroll of the enemies of Turkey, then I am not a democrat!

> . . . If democrat are those who are sapping the foundations of the Republic, then I am not a democrat!

> And I do not wish to be a democrat where such men are called democrat . . . because I am ashamed of sharing with them the same badge.

EPILOGUE

No one familiar with Turkish history of the past half century should be surprised that Turkey suffers from a democratic deficit. The results of the 2007 national elections have led many observers to predict an AKP-dominated era running well into the 2020s. And when the prime minister, in a postelection victory speech, very eloquently reached out to the opposition, promising to be the government of all the Turks, optimism for the future ran high. Even though the corrupt character of the past five years was still living in many memories. But soon after, the regime began to flex its muscles and gave the signal of an all-out effort to cash in and further consolidate the religious character of the society while at the same time continue to line the pockets of its cronies and create a governmental system built on graft, spoils, and patronage. Renewed efforts to legalize the wearing of headscarves in university campuses and accommodating graduates of Imam-Hatip schools during university entrance exams by granting them equivalence to regular state high schools proved, one more time, the Islamists' determination to desecularize the educational reforms of the Kemalist era.

After eight long years, AKP and its personality cult of Erdoğan have brought the country on its knees. It rests on a scaffolding of corruption and on foundations of injustice and police terror. Meanwhile, with record deficits and public debt, the regime's salvation rests on its efforts to privatize and sell the nation's valuable strategic assets to foreign capital. The issue is about the future of the country. If present trade and investment policies are not radically altered, certain industrial sectors will effectively shut their doors; and unemployment, which is already at an intolerable level, will become a national catastrophe.

Today, rescuing the republic from the disaster toward which it is careening must be top priority for anyone who believes in the wisdom of a secular, democratic society, the foundations of which rest upon social justice, and the rule of law.

And yet Turkish Islamic conservatives, even when considered moderate, have never been at peace with a secularism that demands for the withdrawal of religion from the public domain. AKP has, from the very beginning, made determined efforts to fill the cadres of the state bureaucracy with those elements whose credentials were those of pious members of the society. Especially, the inroads made by the brotherhoods—the Naqshibendi and Fethullah Gülen—in penetrating the administrative cadres and the police apparatus have so far been very effective.

What is remarkable is that from the prism of Western modernity, midtwentieth-century Western observers used to laud Atatürk and his Kemalist reforms. But then, a strange thing happened on the way to the twenty-first century. Today, Kemalism has a negative connotation and a pejorative meaning. In an age of politically correct politicians for whom multiculturalism is the solution rather than the problem and when the nation-state is regarded as the obstacle to the bright future of humanity as a single nation ("the end of the nation-state as we know it!"), Kemalism has come to represent all that is wrong with the Turkish society. Now some in the West borrow a page from the Islamist dialectic and accuse Atatürk of "imposing a radical secular revolution on a poor, devout country."[76]

However, there may be a deeper reason well hidden in the pages of history. In fact, twelve years ago, at the height of the PKK's bloody assaults on southeastern civilian population, when their leader Abdullah Öcalan was the toast of Rome and Italy, and when Danielle Mitterand, widow of the former French president and a long-time supporter of the Kurdish cause, was expressing her support for Öcalan and refusing to call terrorism what was the cold-blooded murder of innocent civilians, Steven Kinzer had this to say:[77]

> European Leaders are focusing new attention on the 14-year Kurdish insurgency in Turkey, and many Turks say their interest can best be explained with a single word. It is a word that burns in the Turkish psyche, even though few non-Turks have ever heard it: Sevres.
>
> "I don't like this, but some European countries are longing for a revival of Sevres," Prime Minister Mesut Yılmaz asserted recently . . . His designated successor, Bulent Ecevit, holds the same view. In a warning to European countries that they must not shield Kurdish rebels, he said, "Their ambition for a new Sevres will not be fulfilled."
>
> The Sevres Treaty of 1920, named after the French town where it was signed, ordained that much of what is now Turkey be divided among foreign powers.

Its most valuable and productive regions were apportioned to Greece, Italy, France and Armenia, with the strategic Bosphorus and Dardanelles straits put under international control. Turkey was left only with Ankara and a swath of land around it, much of it mountainous and inhospitable.

That treaty, imposed on the dying Ottoman Empire, set off a burst of patriotic outrage among Turks. Their empire had been shrinking steadily for more than a century, and they considered Sevres their final humiliation.

Now, lately, a voice on tape from another corner of the world reminded the Western establishment that there are some who still remember this period of Middle East history. In one of his recent messages, Osama bin Ladin reminded the people of the Middle East of the Sykes-Picot agreement of 1916. Needless to say, the secret agreement was an early rough draft of Sévres and was initialed between the governments of the United Kingdom and France with the assent of imperial Russia.

The Turkish regime's unfounded optimism regarding Turkey's accession to the EU is matched by its unrealistic approach to the Kurdish problem. It is not clear whether the AKP leadership is so blind as to not appreciate the signals coming from both corners or they are cornered and find no alternative but to pretend that all is well and that happy days are just around the corner.

Listening to the PKK leaders, one might get the impression that Erdoğan is not seriously engaged with the Turkish public about the so-called Kurdish/ Democratic Initiative:

If Turkey had realistic politicians, they would ask themselves and consider why the United States and France do not want a solution to the [Kurdish] problem. Instead, Turkish politicians think, "how nice, these countries are supporting us." They think that with the military, economic, and political support given to them they can dispatch the PKK. But I must respond to them that you cannot eliminate the PKK; this is impossible . . . Those who support Turkey know very well that the PKK cannot be destroyed. Their goal is to ensure that the status quo remains, so that things remain unresolved. It is for this reason that they support Turkey. (Murat Karayılan, acting leader of the PKK, June 27, 2009)[78]

On the other hand, surrendering weapons is not even a subject of discussion. The guerillas [his term for PKK members] will never surrender their weapons. (Duran Kalkan, senior PKK leader, June 23, 2009)[79]

As for the European Union accession iniative, the deception is equally obvious. How can Turkey realistically expect an invitation given the tenor of what the European leaders are saying.

> Accepting Turkey to the EU is out of question. (Angela Merkel [CDU], German chancellor, May 10, 2009, in a conference with French president Nicolas Sarkozy)[80]

> Even now, Turkey's changing role in the Arab world is suspicious. As a full member of the Union, Turkey could not perform its role as a bridge—because a bridge does not belong to one of the sides. (Wolfgang Schauble [CDU], German minister of finance, from his official Web site)[81]

> Turkey's accession is and was an illusion . . . Turkey should recognize that neither the Europeans nor the Turks would accept Turkey's full membership. (Karl-Theodore zu Guttenberg, German minister of defense, October 28, 2009)[82]

As if these problems weren't enough, the country is in the depth of a terrible economic slump. What used to be the scourge of inflation has now been replaced with the scourge of unemployment. The figures for the end of the third quarter are painting a dark and foreboding picture. During the past nine months, unemployment has increased by almost a million. Considering that close to two million unemployed have already given up looking for a job, all in all close to 5.3 million, or about 20 percent of the workforce, are unemployed. Unemployement among young—less than thirty years old—workers is close to 30 percent. And 70 percent of the unemployed are male heads of family.

While the drama of the little man unfolds, a stock market of which 70 percent is owned by foreign investors has registered, during the year 2009, a gain of 97 percent; and the so-called independent media is euphoric at the news, even though it was accompanied by another bit of sobering news: the sum total of the nation debt, including the obligations of national banks to foreign lenders, has reached the unprecedented level of $500 billion. Turkish politicians seem to have forgotten that the nation's constitution calls for social justice for all its citizens!

The Western attitude toward Turkey has always suffered from a certain malaise: the desire to view Turkey as a hired gun to serve the West's strategic interests. This has always provided the backdrop to Turkish-Western relations. It also reflects in the bias analyses and silent approval of the creeping fascism of the Islamist AKP. Let me illustrate the extent of this myopia:

George Friedman is the founder and CEO of STRATFOR, the world's leading private intelligence and forecasting company. In his most recent book, titled *The Next 100 Years*, he makes the following forecast:

> By 2020, Turkey will have emerged as one of the top ten economies in the world . . .

> [It] will be a surging, fairly stable economic and military power in a sea of chaos.

Science fiction is not a favored subject of mine. But the author, at the time, was truly stretching the limits of my imagination. There was more:

> The Islamic world is incapable of uniting voluntarily. It is however, capable of being dominated by a Muslim power. Throughout history, Turkey has been the Muslim power most often able to create an empire out of part of the Islamic world . . .

> During the 2020s, that power will begin to reemerge. Even more than Japan, Turkey will be critical in the confrontation with the Russians . . . As a result, the Turks will be instrumental in America's anti-Russian strategy. The United States will encourage Turkey to press north in the Caucasus and will want Turkish influence in Muslim areas of the Balkans, as well as in the Arab States to the south, to increase."[83]

This, I believe, is a 2020 version of G. W. Bush's Greater Middle East Project (better known in Turkey by its Turkish acronym, BOP). The hope is (as it was then with BOP!) to hire Turkey's services for one more "Greater U.S. Project."

I would not dismiss the possibility of Turkey ending up doing a few things for the United States. Not because, by 2020, Turkey would be a regional power, but rather because, thanks to this wretched Islamist regime, Turkey could be a truly client state with an economy in shambles, a shrinking industrial base with its national resources sold to international corporations, a bankrupt treasury, and an army of semi-illiterate youth.

According to Michael Porter, when nations are ranked in terms of their competitive advantages, the causes of their productivity is no longer their national resources or their labor force but rather their national politics, their educational system, and their innovative spirit.[84]

In terms of its political system's contribution to the economic development of the nation, Turkey ranks 92nd in the world. When the role of its education in the economic development is considered, Turkey slumps even further to 111th. As for its capacity to generate new ideas, the only place Turkey apparently deserves is "very low."

Given the nation's unsolved socioeconomic problems, many had expected that—after five years, by 2007—AKP would have fallen victim to its own corrupt and incompetent practices and its many failures and be terminated by a verdict of the nation's voters. How wrong could one get?

On the contrary, AKP proved to be a party of zombies. Even though it should have been dead long ago, AKP got another lease on life and still continues to breathe, even though it seems to be brain-dead.

It remains to be seen if the sorcerer will be able to provide sufficient supernatural powers to sustain the party of the living dead. For corrupt regimes' worst nightmare is a judgment day here on earth!

NOTES

1. H. C. Armstrong, *Grey Wolf* (London: Penguin Books, 1937).
2. Sedat Sami, *Silent Capitulations: Kemalist Republic under Assault* (New York: iUniverse, 2006).
3. Garrett Ward Sheldon, *Jefferson & Atatürk—Political Philosophies* (New York: Peter Lang, 2000).
4. Sedat Sami, *Silent Capitulations: Kemalist Republic under Assault* (New York: iUniverse, 2006).
5. Ahmed Rashid, *Descent into Chaos* (New York: Penguin Books, 2009).
6. Sedat Sami, *Silent Capitulations: Kemalist Republic under Assault* (New York: iUniverse, 2006).
7. Fareed Zakaria, "The Rise of Illiberal Democracy," *Foreign Affairs* (November 1997).
8. Samuel P. Huntington, *The Third Wave: Democratization in the Late 20th Century* (Norman: University of Oklahoma Press, 1991), 266.
9. Bernard Lewis, "Why Turkey Is the Only Muslim Democracy," *Middle East Quarterly* (March 1994).
10. Stanley Fish, "Monkey Business," *New York Times* (December 2, 2007), http://www.fish.blogs.nytimes.com/2007.
11. Sabrina Tavernise, "Alliances Shift as Turks Weigh a Political Turn," *New York Times* (July 20, 2007).
12. Sabrina Tavernise, "Youthful Voices Stirs Challenges to Secular Turks," *New York Times* (October 13, 2008).
13. Stephen Kinzer, *All the Shah's Men*, (Hoboken, NJ: John Wiley & Sons, 2003), p. 44.
14. Ahmet Taner Kışlalı, "Ben demokrat değilim!" *Cumhuriyet,* (December 27)
15. Stephen Kinzer, "Secular Turks Alarmed by Resurgence of Religion," *New York Times* (February 13, 1997).
16. *Leyla □ahin v. Turkey*, ECHR (Grand Chamber, November 10. 2005).
17. Andrew Higgins, "Turkish Mogul Butts Heads with Premier," *Wall Street Journal* (February 23, 2009).
18. Gareth H. Jenkins, "Between Fact and Fantasy: Turkey's Ergenekon Investigation," *Silk Road Paper* (August 2009).
19. Ibid.

---

20. Fatih Çekirge, "Belge bende," *Hürriyet* (November 23, 2009).
21. Michael Rubin, "Turkey's Putin Deserves to Go," *Wall Street Journal* (June 6, 2008).
22. Aslı Aydıntasbas, "Turkey's War on the Press," *Wall Street Journal* (September 18, 2009).
23. Halil M. Karaveli, "Fusing Statism and Religious Conservatism, Is the AKP Introducing a More Formidable Version of Semi-Authoritarianism?" *Turkey Analyst* 2 (September 14, 2009): 16.
24. Caroline Glick, "Column One: How Turkey Was Lost," http://www.jpost.com (accessed October 16, 2009).
25. Augustus Richard Norton, foreword to *The New Turkish Republic*, by Graham E. Fuller (Washington, DC: United States Institute of Peace, 2008).
26. Graham E. Fuller, *The New Turkish Republic* (Washington, DC: United States Institute of Peace, 2008).
27. Orhan Pamuk, *Charlie Rose Show* (December 28, 2009).
28. M. Hakan Yavuz, *Islamic Political Identity in Turkey* (New York: Oxford University Press, 2005).
29. Mahmood Mamdani, *Saviors and Survivors* (New York: Pantheon Books 2009), 195.
30. Max Weber, *The Protestant Ethic and the Spirit of Capitalism* (Mineola, NY: Dover, 2003), 45.
31. Theodore Roosevelt (speech to the Knights of Columbus, New York City, October 12, 1915).
32. Fatih Altaylı, "Bu ülke bölünecek," *Habertürk gazetesi* (November 18, 2009).
33. Ertuğrul Özkök, "Izmir sivil faşist mi," *Hürriyet* (November 26, 2009).
34. Hasan Cemal, *Kürtler* (Istanbul: Doğan Kitap, April 2003), 544.
35. Abdülmelik Fırat was then a deputy from the True Path Party (DYP, now defunct) and presently represents AKP in parliament.
36. Ismet Sezgin served as president of the Turkish parliament and later was NATO's Afghanistan representative.
37. Hasan Cemal, *Kürtler* (Doğan Kitap, April 2003), 543.
38. Ibid., 544.
39. The Constitution of the Republic of Turkey (English), http://*www.hri.org/docs/ turkey* (ibid., 544).
40. "PKK den yedi çözüm önerisi" [Seven steps for a solution from PKK] *Kandil-b□A haber merkezi*4, http://news.bianet.org/bianet (accessed November 10, 2009).
41. Michael Burleigh, *Earthly Powers: The Clash of Religion and Politics in Europe, from the French Revolution to the Great War* (New York: Harper Perennial, 2007).
42. Patrick J. Buchanan, *Day of Reckoning* (New York: St. Martin Press 2007), 169.
43. Strobe Talbot, "The Birth of the Global Nation," *Time* (July 20, 1992), 70.

44. British Foreign Office document 371/6502/E.3557.

45. British Foreign Office document 371/6504/E.8519. R. C. Craige, British Embassy, to Lord Curzon, No.722, of July 13, 1921.

46. Hovhannes Katchaznouni, "Dashnagtzoutiun Has Nothing to Do Anymore" (report submitted to the 1923 Party Convention, Istanbul: Kaynak Yayınları, June 2007).

47. *Mschak,* no. 271 (1914). Cited by Marents, "Litso Arsyaskogo Smenohovstva," *Bolchevik Zakavakazya,* No. 3-4 (1928), 89.

48. Gunter Lewy, "Revisiting the Armenian Genocide," *Middle East Quarterly* (Fall 2005).

49. Edward J. Erickson, "Armenian Massacres: New Records Undercut Old Blame—Reexamining History," *Middle East Quarterly* (Summer 2006).

50. Norman Stone, "Armenian Story Has Another Side," *Chicago Tribune* (October 16, 2007).

51. Charlie Rose Web site, http://www.charlierose.com (December 8, 2008).

52. "Hillary Clinton Supports Adoption of Armenian Genocide Resolution," ANCA (January 24, 2008).

53. "Aznavour toprak istedi Başpatrik ise tazminat," *Hürriyet* (November 2, 2009).

54. Edgar Hilsenrath, *Das März en vom letzten Gedanken* (Berlin: Deutscher Taschenbuch Verlag, 2006).

55. Ahmet Davutoğlu, *Stratejik derinlik* (Istanbul: Küre Yayınları, 2009), 592.

56. *Hürriyet* (March 3, 2009).

57. Cem Ryan, "The Trial of Mustafa Kemal Atatürk, Part I," http://forreasonsunknown-cem.blogspot.com.

58. Şükrü Kızılot, "Babalar ve çocukları" [Fathers and sons] *Hürriyet* (July 17, 2007).

59. Şükrü Kızılot, "Gemiler, fabrikalar, ve villalar" [Ships, factories and villas] *Hürriyet* (July 19, 2007).

60. Şükrü Kızılot, "5 yıl oldu hâlâ pırlanta KDV'si tartışılıyor" [It has been 5 years, still debating diamond's VAT] *Hürriyet* (February 10, 2009).

61. Larry Diamond, "The Democratic Rollback," *Foreign Affairs* (March-April 2008), 43.

62. Ismet Berkan, "Memleketin birinde" [In a certain country] *Radikal* (September 10, 2008).

63. Ismet Berkan, "Memleketin birinde: Becerikli Abdullah Bey" [In a certain country: Talented Abdullah Bey] *Radikal* (September 11, 2008).

64. Ismet Berkan, "Memleketin birinde: Banka için birbirine giren ekip" [In a certain country: A team fighting each other for a bank] *Radikal* (September 12, 2008).

65. Elektrik Mühendisleri Odası (EMO), "Fener Işığında Gölge Oyunları" [Shadow plays under the lighthouse] (December 4, 2009).

66. Ali Bulaç, http://www.bilgivehikmet.com (accessed January 26, 2006).

67. Ali Bulaç, http://www.bilgivehikmet.com (accessed February 11, 2006).

68. "İşbaşaran zehir zemberek," http://www.milliyet.com.tr (accessed December 26, 2009).

69. Kurt Vonnegut, *A Man Without a Country* (New York: Seven Stories Press, 2005).

70. Fareed Zakaria, "The Rise of Illiberal Democracy," *Foreign Affairs* (November 1997).

71. Ibid.

72. "Şener'den AKP'ye eleştiri," http://www.milliyet.com.tr (accessed December 28, 2009).

73. Ernst Mandel, *Late Capitalism* (London: Verso, 1978), 372.

74. Ronald Inglehardt and Christian Welzel, "How Development Leads to Democracy," *Foreign Affairs* (March-April 2009).

75. Ahmet Taner Kışlalı, ibid.

76. Sabrina Tavernise, "In Complex Times, Turkey Seeks a Reassuring Face," *New York Times* (January 16, 2008).

77. Steven Kinzer, "Turks See Throwback to Partition in Europe's Focus on Kurds," *New York Times* (December 7, 1998).

78. Soner Cagaptay, "In Their Own Words: PKK Leaders on Peace, Dialogue, and the United States," *Policy Watch #1561* (July 29, 2009).

79. Ibid.

80. Soner Cagaptay, "Germany's New Cabinet on Turkey's EU Accession," *Policy Watch #1596* (October 30, 2009).

81. Ibid.

82. Ibid.

83. George Friedman, *The Next 100 Years* (New York: Doubleday, 2009), 145.

84. Michael Porter, *Competitive Advantage of Nations* (New York: Harvard Business Review, March 3, 2009).

SELECT BIBLIOGRAPHY

Archives Reports

National Archives, Nixon Presidential Material. NSC Files, Country Files, Middle East, Greece, Vol IV, Box 594. Secret.

National Archives, RG 59, Transcripts of Henry Kissinger's Staff Meetings, Entry 5177, Box 5, Secretary's Staff Conference. Secret.

Ford Library, National Security Advisor, Memoranda of Conversations, Washington, June 26, 1975. Box 13, 6/26/75. Confidential.

Library of Congress, Manuscript Division, Kissinger Papers, Box CL272, Memoranda of Conversations, November 13, 1974. Chronological File. Secret. Drafted by Eagleton and approved in S/S on November 16, 1974

European Court of Human Rights (echr.coe.int) Grand Chamber Judgment : Leyla Şahin v. Turkey 10.11.2005

U.S. Department of State. Bureau of Democracy, Human Rights, and Labor International Religious Freedom Report 2009 (Oct. 26, 2009) (www.state. gov)

Freedom House. Report on Freedom of the Press-Turkey 2009 (freedomhouse. org)

Commission of the European Communities-Turkey 2009 Progress Report (ec. europa.eu)

World Economic Forum: The Global Gender Gap Index Report 2009

Published Sources

(in English)

The Abant Platform: Final Declarations. Istanbul: Journalists and Writers Foundation. 1999, 2000.

Abramowitz, Morton and Henri J. Barkey. "Turkey's Transformers: The AKP Sees Big. *Foreign Affairs* (November-December 2009).

Aras, Bülent. *Turkey and the Greater Middle East*. Istanbul: TASAM, 2004.

Aras, Bülent. "Turkish Islam's Moderate Face." *Middle East Quarterly* (September 1998).

Armstrong, H. C. *Grey Wolf*. London: Penguin Books, 1937.

Atasoy, Yıldız. "Islamic Revivalism & the Nation-State Project." Univ. of Toronto: yatasoy@epas.utoronto.ca.

Burleigh, Michael. *Earthly Powers: The Clash of Religion and Politics in Europe.* New York: Harper, 2007.

Buchanan, Patrick. *Day of Reckoning.* New York: St. Martin, 2007.

Cem, Ismail. *Turkey in the New Century.* Nicosia: Rustem, 2001.

Choamsky, Noam. *Failed States.* New York: Metropolitan Books, 2006.

Cornell, Swante E. and Halil Magnus Karaveli. "Prospects for a 'Torn' Turkey: A Secular and Unitary Future?" Central Asia-Caucasus Institute Silk Road paper, October 2008.

Friedman, George. *The Next 100 Years.* New York: Doubleday, 2009.

Fromkin, David. *A Peace to End All Peace.* New York: Holt, 1998.

Fuller, Graham E. *The New Turkish Republic.* Washington, DC: United States Institute of Peace, 2008.

Fuller, Graham. "Turkey's Strategic Model: Myths and Realities." *Washington Quarterly* (Summer 2004).

Goodwin, Jason. *Lord of the Horizons.* New York: Holt, 1998.

Gordon, Philip H. and Omer Taşpınar. *Winning Turkey.* Washington, DC: Brookings Institute, 2008.

Göl, Ayla. "Imagining the Turkish Nation through Othering Armenians." *Nations & Nationalism* 11 (2005).

Gürün, Kamuran. *The Armenian File: The Myth of Innocence Exposed.* Istanbul: Technical Univ., 2001.

Huntington, S. P. *The Third Wave: Democratization in the Late 20th Century.* Normal: Univ. of Oklahoma, 1991.

Horne, Alistair. *A Savage War of Peace.* New York: New York Review of Books, 2006.

Hirsi, Ayan. "Don't Disarm Secularism." *New Perspectives Quarterly* (Summer 2007).

Hitchens, Christopher. *Hostage to History: Cyprus from the Ottomans to Kissinger.* London: Verso, 1997.

Inglehardt, Ronald and Christian Welzel. "How Development Leads to Democracy." *Foreign Affairs* (March-April 2009).

Jang, Ji-Hyang. "The Politics of Islamic Banks in Turkey." Midwest Political Science Assoc. Chicago (2003). http://www.gov.utexas.edu/content/research_paper/midwest_903/jangmpsal03.pdf.

Jung, Dietrich and Wolfangs Piccolo. *Turkey at the Crossroads: Ottoman Legacies & a Greater Middle East*, London: Zed Books, 2001.

Kaplan, Robert D. *The Coming Anarchy.* New York: Vintage Books, 2001.

Karaveli, Halil M. "Fusing Statism and Religious Conservatism: Is the AKP Introducing a More Formidable Version of Semi-Authoritarianism?" *Turkey Analyst*2, no.16.

Karaveli, Halil M. "Turkish Society Increasingly Marked by Intolerance toward 'the Other'." *Turkey Analyst* (January 30, 2009).

Katchaznouni, Hovhannes. *Dashnagtzoutiun Has Nothing to Do Anymore*. Istanbul: Kaynak, 2007.

Kinross, Lord. *Atatürk—The Rebirth of a Nation*. London: Weidenfeld & Nicholson, 1964.

—. *The Ottoman Centuries*. New York: Morrow Quill, 1997.

Kinzer, Stephen. *All the Shah's Men*. Hoboken: Wiley, 2003.

Kinzer, Stephen. *Crescent and Star*. New York: Farrar, 2001.

Klein, Naomi. *The Shock Doctrine:The Rise of Disaster Capitalism*. New York: Metropolitan Books, 2007.

Köprülü, Fuad. *The Origin of the Ottoman Empire*. New York: New York State Univ., 1992.

Laçiner, Sedat. "Turkish Islam and Turkey's EU Membership." *Journal of Turkish Weekly*, July 15, 2005.

Landau, Jakob M. *Pan-Turkism in Turkey*. London: Hurst, 1981.

—. *The Politics of Pan Islam*. Oxford: Clanderon, 1994.

Laqueur, Walter. *The Last Days of Europe*. New York: St. Martin, 2007.

Lewis, Bernard. *The Crisis of Islam—Holy War and Unholy Terror*. Random House, 2004.

Lewy, Guenter. *The Armenian Massacres in Ottoman Turkey (A Disputed Genocide)*. Salt Lake City: Univ. of Utah Press, 2005.

Mamdani, Mahmood. *Good Muslim, Bad Muslim*. New York: Doubleday, 2005.

Mamdani, Mahmood. *Saviors and Survivors*. New York: Pantheon Books, 2009.

Mandel, Ernst. *Late Capitalism*. London: Verso, 1978.

Mango, Andrew. *Atatürk*. New York: Overlook, 2000.

—. *The Turks Today*. New York: Overlook, 2004.

—. *Turkey and the War on Terror: For Forty Years We Fought Alone*. Florence: Routledge, 2005.

Mardin, Şerif. *The Genesis of Young Ottoman Thought*. Princeton: Princeton Univ. Press, 1962.

Marcus, Aliza. *Blood and Belief: The PKK and the Kurdish Fight for Independence*. New York: NYU Press, 2007.

Mastny, Vojtech and R. Craig Nation. *Turkey Between East & West*. Boulder: Westview, 1996.

McCarthy, Justin et al. *The Armenian Rebellion at Van*. Salt Lake City: Univ. of Utah Press, 2006.

McCarthy, Justin. *Death & Exile: The Ethnic Cleansing of Ottoman Muslims 1821-1922*. Princeton: Darwin, 1999.

McCarthy, Justin. *The Ottoman Peoples and the End of Empire*. New York: Oxford Univ. Press, 2001.

Nasr, Vali. *Forces of Fortune*. New York: Free Press, 2009

Pope, Nicole. *Turkey Unveiled*. New York: Overlook, 1998.

Porter, Michael. *Competitive Advantage of Nations*. New York: Harward Business Review, 2009.

Robins, Philip. *Suits and Uniforms:Turkish Foreign Policy Since the Cold War.* Seattle: Univ. of Washington Press, 2003.

Sheldon, Garrett Ward. *Jefferson & Atatürk: Political Philosophies*. New York: Lang, 2000.

Sami, Sedat. *Silent Capitulations: Kemalist Republic under Assault*. New York: iUniverse, 2006.

Rashid, Ahmed. *Descent into Chaos*. New York: Penguin Books, 2009.

Rustow, D. A. *Turkey: America's Forgotten Ally*. New York: Council on Foreign Relations, 1987.

Sharon-Krespin, Rachel. "Fethullah Gülen's Grand Ambition." *Middle East Quarterly* (Winter 2009).

Thornton, Bruce. *Decline and Fall—Europe's Slow-Motion Suicide*. New York: Encounter Books, 2007.

Tripp, Charles. "All (Muslim) Politics Is Local." *Foreign Affairs* (September-October 2009).

Védrine, Hubert. *History Strikes Back—How States, Nations, and Conflicts Are Shaping the 21st Century*. New York: Brookings Institution, 2008.

Vidino, Lorenzo. "The Muslim Brotherhood's Conquest of Europe." *Middle East Quarterly* (Winter 2005).

Vonnegut, Kurt. *A Man without a Country*. New York: Seven Stories, 2005.

Warner, Geoffrey. "The United States and the Cyprus Crisis of 1974." *International Affairs* 85 (2009).

Weber, Max. *The Protestant Ethic and the Spirit of Capitalism*. Mineola: Dover Publications, 2003.

Wheatcroft, Andrew. *The Ottomans*. London: Penguin Books, 1995.

White, Jenny B. "The End of Islamism? Turkey's Muslimhood Model." *Remaking Muslim Politics:Pluralism, Contestation, Democratization*. ed, Robert W. Hefner, Princeton: Princeton Univ. Press, 2005.

Wittes, Tamara Cofman. "Islamist Parties: Three Kinds of Movements." *Journal of Democracy* 19, no.3 (July 2008).

Woods, Ellen Meiksins. *Empire of Capital*. London: Verso, 2003.

Yavuz, M. Hakan. "Towards an Islamic Liberalism?: The Nurcu Movement and Fethullah Gülen." *Middle East Journal* (Winter 1999).

Yavuz, M. Hakan and John Esposito, eds. *Turkish Islam and the Secular State: The Gülen Movement*. Washington, DC: Georgetown Univ. Press, 2002.

Yavuz, M. Hakan. *Islamic Political Identity in Turkey.* New York: Oxford Univ. Press, 2005.

Published Sources
(in Turkish)

Akçura, Yusuf. *Türkçülü□ün Tarihi.* Istanbul: Kaynak, 1998.

Aydemir, Şevket Süreyya. *Tek Adam.* 3 vols. Istanbul: Remzi, 1963.

Borak, Sadi. *Atatürk'ün Resmi Yayınlara Girmemi□ Söylev Demeç Yazı□ma ve Söyle□ileri.* Istanbul: Kaynak, 1998.

Bölük, Mehmet. *El Tayyip.* Istanbul: Toplumsal Dönüşüm, 2002.

Cemal, Hasan. *Kürtler.* Istanbul: Doğan Kitap, 2003.

Çetin, Kaya. *□eriat mı? Ça□da□ ya□am mı?* Istanbul: Berfin, 2004.

Çizmeli, Şevket. *Menderes Demokrasi Yıldızı?* Ankara: Arkadaş, 2007.

Davutoğlu, Ahmet. *Stratejik Derinlik: Türkiyenin Uluslararası konumu.* Istanbul: Küre Yayın, 2001.

Erkin, Aytun. *Fethullah Hoca'nın □ifreleri.* Istanbul: Kaynak, 2005.

Fırat, Gökçe et al. *Yeni Sömürgecili□e kar□ı Yeni Milliyetçilik.* Istanbul: Ileri, 2004.

Hablemitoğlu, Necip. *Köstebek.* Istanbul: Toplumsal Dönüşüm, 2003.

Kışlalı, Ahmet Taner. *Ben Demokrat De□ilim!* Ankara: Imge, 1999.

Kaleli, Lutfi. *Sıvas Katliamı ve □eriat.* Istanbul: Alev, 1994.

Kongar, Emre. *Demokrasimizle Yüzle□mek.* Istanbul: Remzi, 2007.

Mango, Andrew. *Türkiyenin Terörle Sava□ı.* Istanbul: Doğan, 2005.

Manisalı, Erol. *Sömürgele□en Türkiye.* Istanbul: Derin, 2004.

Mumcu, Uğur. *Tarikat, Siyaset, Ticaret.* Ankara: um.ag, 1997.

Özakıncı, Cengiz. *Türkiyenin Siyasi □ntiharı.* Istanbul: Otopsi, 2005.

Özden, Yekta Güngör. *Atatürk ve Atatürkçülük.* Istanbul: Ileri, 2003.

Öztürk, Yaşar Nuri. *Allah ile Aldatmak.* Istanbul: Yeni Boyut, 2008.

Perinçek, Doğu. *Mafyokrasi.* Istanbul: Kaynak, 2005.

—. *Tayyip Erdo□an'ın Yüce Divan Dosyası: Haçlı Irtica.* Istanbul: Kaynak, 2008.

Savaş, Vural. *Türkiye Cumhuriyeti Çökerken.* Ankara: Bilgi, 2004.

—. *Satılmı□ların Ekonomisi.* Ankara: Bilgi, 2002.

Şimşir, Bilal N. *Ermeni Meselesi. 1774-2005.* Ankara: Bilgi, 2005.

Velidedeoğlu, Meriç. *Demokrasiden Teokrasiye mi?* Istanbul: Cumhuriyet Kitap, 2008.

Yanardağ, Merdan. *Bir ABD Projesi Olarak AKP.* Istanbul: Siyah Beyaz, 2007.

—. *Fethullah Gülen Hareketinin Perde Arkası.* Istanbul: Siyah Beyaz, 2008.

—. *Medya Nasıl Ku□atıldı?* Istanbul: Siyah Beyaz, 2008.

Yavuz, H. ve J. L. Esposito. *Laik Devlet ve Fethullah Gülen.* Istanbul: Gelenek.

Media
(in foreign languages: consulted or referred to)

The articles *the* and *le* have not been considered in the alphabetical sequence.

The Brookings Institution (brookings.edu)
Carnegie Endowment for International Peace (carnegieendowment.org)
Center for Security Policy (centerforsecuritypolicy.org)
Center for Strategic and International Studies (csis.org)
Central Asia-Caucasus Institute Silk Road Studies (silkroadstudies.org)
Chatham House (chathamhouse.org.uk)
Chicago Tribune (chicagotribune.com)
Christian Science Monitor (csmonitor.com)
Defense News (defensenews.org)
Economist (ec.com)
Euro-Atlantic Quarterly (eaq.sk)
Fethullah Gülen (fgulen.org)
Le Figaro (lefigaro.fr)
Financial Times (ft.com)
Foreign Affairs (foreignaffairs.org)
Foreign Policy (foreignpolicy.com)
Frankfurter Allgemeine
Hudson Institute Center for Eurasian Policy (hudson.org)
Guardian (guardian.co.uk)
The Jamestown Foundation (jamestown.org)
Jerusalem Post (jpost.com)
Los Angeles Times (latimes.com)
Middle East Quarterly (meforum.org)
Le Monde (lemonde.fr)
New York Times (nytimes.com)
Sunday Times (timesonline.com)
The Washington Institute for Near East Policy (washingtoninstitute.org)
Washington Post (washingtonpost.com)
Wall Street Journal (wsj.com)
Yedioth Ahronoth (ynetnews.com)

Media
(in Turkish: consulted or referred to)

Ak□am (aksam.com.tr)
Aydınlık (aydinlik.com.tr)

Birgün (birgun.net)
Bugün (bugun.com.tr)
Cumhuriyet (cumhuriyet.com.tr)
Haber türk (htgazete.com.tr)
Hürriyet (hurriyet.com.tr)
Milli gazette (milligazete.com.tr)
Milliyet (milliyet.com.tr)
Radikal (radikal.com.tr)
Sabah (sabah.com.tr)
Star gazete (stargazete.com)
Taraf (taraf.com.tr)
Tercüman (tercuman.com.tr)
Türkiye (turkiye.com.tr)
Vakit (vakit.com.tr)
Vatan (gazetevatan.com)
Yeni □afak (yenisafak.com.tr)
Zaman (zaman.com.tr)

Index

C

Cagaptay, Soner, 90
Calvin, 42
capitulations, 17-18, 87, 94
Caucasus, 33, 44, 50, 52, 85, 92, 96
CBS, 60
Cemal, Hasan, 45
Central Asia-Caucasus Institute, 33
Charlie Rose Show, 39
Chechens, 44
Çiller, Tansu, 18, 24
Circassia, 52
Clinton, Hillary, 57, 89
CNN Türk, 64
Constitutional Court, Turkish, 30-1
corporations, multinational, 19, 24
corruption, 25, 28, 32, 35, 38, 42, 64,
    66-70, 72, 75, 80-1
Costello, Jerry, 25
Council of Europe, 31
Crimea, 52
Curzon, Lord, 53, 89
Customs Union, 18
Cyprus, 50, 57, 59, 92, 94

D

Daniştay, 75
Dardanelles, 54, 83
Dashnagtzoutiun, 53-4, 89, 93
Davutoğlu, Ahmet, 60
Declaration on Human Rights in Islam,
    37
Demirel, Süleyman, 24
democracy, 19, 21-2, 24-7, 30, 33-4,
    37-8, 40, 42, 71, 74-5, 77, 79-80,
    87, 90-2, 94
  functioning, 22, 25, 30, 42
  illiberal, 19, 21-2, 75, 87, 90
  Muslim, 24, 34, 87, 94

religiously pluralistic, 22
secular, 22, 27, 30, 77
sham, 80
Democratic Initiative, 48
Deniz Feneri, 66-7
Diamond, Larry, 67, 89
Diyarbakir, 66
Doğan, Aydin, 33
Doğan Media Group, 32
DTP, 48-9, 76
Durbin, Dick, 25

E

Ecevit, Bülent, 45
Economist, 25, 96
economy, free market, 24, 28
ecumenical, 60
elections, Turkish, 25
empire, 17-18, 28-30, 44-5, 51-2, 56-8,
    60, 83, 85, 93-4
  Greek Orthodox, 60
  Ottoman, 17-18, 30, 44, 51-2, 56-8, 60,
    83, 93-4
  Russian, 52
Erbakan, 24, 40-1
Erdoğan
  Ahmet Burak, 65
  Recep Tayyip, 19
Erez, Yalim, 45
Ergenekon, 33-4, 64, 87
Erickson, Edward J., 55, 89
Erivan Province, 52
Ermiş, F., 32
Erzurum, 58
European Convention on Human Rights,
    30-1
European Court of Human Rights, 30-1,
    41, 91
European Union, 18, 28, 30, 50, 56, 59,
    61, 84